PLAYING LIFE BY EAR

PLAYING LIFE BY EAR

Notes from Eighty-Nine Years of Living, Learning, Laughing, Loving, and Believing

Doris Markland

PLAYING LIFE BY EAR
NOTES FROM EIGHTY-NINE YEARS OF LIVING, LEARNING, LAUGHING, LOVING, AND BELIEVING

iUniverse books may be ordered through booksellers or by contacting:

iUniverse
1663 Liberty Drive
Bloomington, IN 47403
www.iuniverse.com
1-800-Authors (1-800-288-4677)

ISBN: 978-1-4917-5992-9 (sc)
ISBN: 978-1-4917-5991-2 (e)

Library of Congress Control Number: 2015901567

Print information available on the last page.

iUniverse rev. date: 03/16/2015

To my children,
Sara, John, and Tom Markland,
who saw me through my life,
with special thanks to Sara,
who saw me through
this book.

CONTENTS

PREFACE

This book is not the story of my life but the stories of my life, the kind you share with friends, the kind that linger until you figure out their meaning. It is also a collection of my poetry, some that I wrote for Hallmark or for magazines but more that I wrote for fun.

The stories are true. They are memories not just of what I lived, day to day, but what I thought and what I felt. The mind can be a busy place, but what circulates there goes nowhere if it isn't also in your heart. Actually, any desire I ever had to communicate or to accomplish or to inspire began in the feeling part of me, and my intellect then joined in to do the work and make it come true.

As you read, I hope that my insights will lead you to insights of your own. I shall be so happy if you find even one thing in my book that has meaning for you.

LIVING

Playing by Ear

They say practice makes perfect, but I say that's conditional. You have to want to practice. You have to practice the thing that's right for you.

I received my first piano as a gift under the Christmas tree. It was probably twelve inches long, pale green with white keys. I sat down right there by the tree and played all the Christmas songs we had been singing. I played them perfectly. I was four. The adults were amazed.

So my mother bought a used piano, and of course I was taking piano lessons as soon as I was old enough, playing the scales and exercises over and over and over—and then the assigned nondescript song. I listened for the kitchen door, and when I knew my mother had gone out to work in the garden, I closed my books and played for me. I played the songs we sang in school, the songs we sang in church, the songs I heard on the radio ... and the songs I heard in my head. As for the lessons, I continued them for years, but beyond a certain point I stalled, and instruction was pointless.

On the playground, I was the last one chosen for any team—not because I wasn't popular but because I was small and lacked the spirit of competition. Still, I did make the girls' basketball team in high school. I was thrilled because it got me out of the ugly, green, belted uniforms we wore for gym class and into the cute, white satin suits of the team. We practiced every day and played games on the weekend. Coach put me in sometimes to spell one of the stars, but I was soon back on the bench.

It should have come as no surprise when, at the beginning of my senior year, he called me into his office and I learned I was on the team only to make the numbers and that I was being replaced by a sophomore who had just moved into town. I was crushed, but my parents were pleased. Years later they told me how they dreaded those moments when I was sent into the game. Years of practice had made no difference. I was not a competitor. I played too nice.

I went to a small but very good college, and because I was offered a minimum music scholarship, I pursued a music major and was selected to sing in their fine touring choir. But we didn't tour in 1942, because of WWII. Still, I enjoyed the rehearsals and the local concerts, until one day the director took me aside. He was making some changes and told me I was one soprano he wouldn't need. Curses. In school, studying music, and in all the hours of rehearsals, I had never improved.

I switched to a more general course and was required to have hours in sports. I chose tennis and passed it only because I memorized the rules. Swimming I passed because I could finally make it from one side of the pool to the other. I tried golf and found I couldn't even beat myself.

As an adult, I played bridge. For years I played in a social foursome, in a contract duplicate club, and sometimes on Wednesdays I played duplicate at the country club after lunch. I liked it because it got me out of the house, the food was good, and I was with friends. It was a long time, however, before I noticed how often a partner was tapping her fingers on the table, waiting for my play because I was listening to the background music or I was watching a robin in the tree outside the window.

One day it came to me clearly. I was not good at bridge, and I wasn't getting any better. I made calls to opt out and never played bridge again. It felt good, and now I had time for other things.

With friends socially, we often gathered around the piano, and I played the songs they wanted to sing. I played by ear, and it wasn't perfect, but after all, their singing was not perfect either. They were singing by ear.

In the late fifties or early sixties, I found some success at contests sponsored by companies who asked us to tell why we liked their product in twenty-five words or less. I loved to write, and now for fun I researched how to write greeting cards. It was something I could do at home while the kids were in school. In the quiet of my house, I could hear. And I wrote what I heard. In time, my cards were on several counters, especially Hallmark's, and eventually my cards bore my name. Not to say this had not taken practice but to say that the practice brought a certain amount of result. Particularly as I learned to listen.

It was a while before it came through to me that in all areas of my life I did best when I made use of my inner wisdom, my inner inspiration, my inner guidance for direction. I do believe my muse is an angel, or perhaps

I have several angels who move into my aura to help me when needed, particularly to help me when I'm on track—my track.

No doubt about it. Life is a learning experience. There are things I must do, things I can do, and things I love to do. But I am happiest and most successful when I'm in my feelings, when I'm alert to inner promptings, when I'm playing life by ear.

I have done a lot of things in my eighty-nine years, but nothing tops my performance in 1929, on Christmas Eve, when I was four.

Rain on My Parade, Please

It comes quickly, gray clouds bubbling up on the horizon, a sudden wind, and then an eerie hush that stills the birds, those that haven't headed south. I step outside to feel the first large splats of rain and then back into the shelter of the open garage to watch the force build.

Straight down at first, the drops become silvery streams, slanting now in sheets that strike and power-wash the driveway, then turn tame and curl in rivers down the street, taking flaky autumn leaves and any last hints of summer.

I stand in the doorway, thrilled, breathing in the delicious scent of nature's shower, shivering a little but not from the cold.

I'm reliving one of the strongest memories from my childhood in the thirties, the dry years, when rain was so desperately needed in the Midwest. Farmers watched the sky day by day, shaking their heads when rogue clouds built and frayed away, one wisp at a time, leaving us still with the plague of red dust that wasn't even ours.

But then came a day when the sky grew angry and rumbled with promise. We felt the tension, and so did our animals, when streaks of lightning came. The family gathered on the lawn, unbelieving, then rejoicing at the first raindrop, laughing and running in circles, soaked to the skin as it began to pour. I had never seen my parents so happy.

The feeling of those moments registered with me as deliverance, the opening of a window of hope. Rain meant relief from the heat. It meant prosperity for the crops. It meant a cleansing of the lawns, the roads, the atmosphere … and the soul.

From then on, mental images of certain rainy days were captured and stored in my mind as special.

Picture: On a rainy day, I could play outside in my oldest clothes, squeezing mud between bare toes, running into new ponds in the driveway, deep lakes in the hollows of the lawn, laughing, rain slicking my hair and streaming down the length of me. *Click.*

Picture: My fiancé, home from the war, arriving unexpectedly to take me to work. He comes to the door with an umbrella and a large bouquet of lilacs, covered with droplets and smelling like heaven. We dash through the rain, holding hands. *Click.*

Picture: My son, at five, in yellow slicker and hat, turns to wave good-bye as he trudges off to kindergarten, sloshing through September puddles, grinning with pride in his new independence. *Click.*

Every picture that I saved is there in my permanent mental hard drive, and on rainy days, I bring them up and look at them. It's a nice feeling.

Other pictures that didn't turn out so good, like the time I ran out of gas on the freeway in the middle of a storm, or the time the sky poured on my yard sale, those were not keepers, and eventually I deleted them.

I remember a cartoon character saying a rainy day is a good time to put on some music, drink hot tea, and look out the window. It is also a good time to clean out a closet, read a good book, simmer a stew, or maybe just do nothing!

It's raining. You must stay in unless you must go to work in the rain, and that can be promising too. I think of all the movies in which the star met someone interesting in a downpour on his way to work … or danced down the street with his umbrella.

Spring rain may be refreshing, but fall rain comes with subtle colors and a distinctive mood. I'd call the color golden (think wet leaves and harvest moon). I'd call the mood pensive. One is more likely to go in than out when rain is streaming on the glass.

Soft and sentimental as it may be, autumn rain must be the instrument, together with the wind, that strips October's trees of their last dangling leaves, baring limbs to arch against the background of November's pink and gray sunsets.

Soon no more rain, but maybe lots of snow.

We'll hunker down until it rains again.

I love the rain.

DeKarmalizing

We'd like to be lady
And lord of the manor
With acres of land
That we own free of debt.
We'd like to be smarter
And thinner and tanner
And think that old age
Isn't creeping up yet.
We'd like all our kids
To be handsome, athletic,
And brainy enough
To place first on the list
And then to go on
To executive stardom
And marry just once
To the best one they kissed.
But life has a way
Of repeating a pattern,
So apples that fall
Remain close to the tree,
And the children we raise,
Though all smart
And good looking,
Repeat all the faults
That as children they see.
So we watch for improvement
As age comes upon us
And hope that our kids
Will reverse all the trends
And ease all the burdens
Of family karma …
Make history, maybe,
At least make amends.

My Little Dumplings and Diversity

My grown children sometimes refer to me as June Cleaver. You remember June Cleaver? That was Beaver's mother on the *Leave It to Beaver* TV show.

I'm afraid I do have some things in common with June Cleaver. I looked fairly presentable while I ran the home and planned the meals and cooked from scratch and oversaw the table. No doubt I asked the children questions about their day, and I watched to see that they ate properly.

The problem is that after umpteen years as chairman of their food committee, it's very hard to resign from that position, even though the little ones are big ones now and their pins on my Google Earth are far apart and far from me.

When they come home to visit, they still, nearing middle age, roll their eyes (a skill perfected by the Baby Boomers) over this phenomenon. They make jokes about the Midwest being the Jell-O belt and refer to us as the food-pushers. Casseroles are suspect. They decline seconds on any dish and remind us of their peculiarities … their vegetarianism, their sugar-free or fat-free diet, or the fact that they simply don't have time to eat. It is like a dagger to my heart. But still I fuss and stew, if you will forgive the culinary reference, because I am so programmed to feed those I brought in.

When they married and brought a new family member home for a visit, that's when things became complicated. My son-in-law is a meat-and-potatoes kind of guy. He eats little fruit, and the only vegetable he likes is asparagus, but it must be cooked until it's gray and limp. His wife, my daughter, is a vegetarian and eats no meat, fish, or poultry but does eat most vegetables. She likes them steamed, and just barely. But, good heavens, no asparagus! And that's only one of the families I must consider at Thanksgiving or Christmastime.

Our home, which once held two adults and three children, now becomes at times a gathering place for everyone, including the grandchildren and great-grandchildren. Among this merry conglomerate are three who will not eat nuts, one who is allergic to chicken, and five who gag at the thought of onions. So we cook two dishes, one with and one without.

Then there is the bachelor who will neither talk nor eat until he has Starbucked himself into consciousness. We put the omelets on hold and wait for him to catch up.

When the children were small, we held them to things like "don't talk with your mouth full," "don't play with your food," and, most important, "you must take some of everything." "If you think you don't like peas," we said, "you may take only one pea, but you may not skip the peas." Our saying was that all foods are good, but for each of us some are just better than others. When they left our home, they were about as free of prejudice as one can be, so I can see it is the world that is testing them.

It's like life. We give our children rules to live by until they are mature enough to set their own. Along the way, they experiment, and every now and then they check home base to get their bearings and to make certain comparisons as they learn and grow in their own patterns.

As parents, we watch, and we shake or nod our heads. It isn't always easy. Still, there are those times when no one is looking. A grown son peeks into the cookie jar and, finding it empty, says, "But, Mom … you *knew* I was coming!"

A grandson slips up behind me at the kitchen sink, throws his big arms around me, and says "No one makes gravy like you do, Grandma."

The daughter calls frantically for recipes for company. "But, please, none with Jell-O."

As mothers, we do say good-bye when our children grow up and leave the home. We just never quite shut the door.

Palmer Method

I was reminded recently of the exercises my generation lived through while learning how to write cursive. Not just how to write but how to write well. One of the tools we used was the Palmer Method of handwriting. We did not use pencils for this, and we didn't as yet have fountain pens, much less ballpoint pens. Ours was a wooden stem into which we placed a small, metal pen-point (which needed replacing often). And then we dipped the pen into a bottle of ink. Often.

In this type of writing, we did not write with our fingers but with our arms. Pen in hand, we placed the underarm on the desk and rolled on that fat/muscle to make the motion of writing, which was either up and down or around and around. For practice, we did push-and-pulls and ovals, holding the hand still and moving the arm. If you try this, you will see it is the exact movements we use to make numbers and letters. We filled pages of these scrolls and letters and numbers and in time were required to submit a perfect page, and we then received a beautiful blue and gold pin to wear. That was in the thirties.

One day, some years ago, as I stood patiently ironing a stack of my husband's shirts, I realized that again I was making those same two movements, either up and down or around and around. It came together in a poem, which I promptly wrote when I left the ironing board for my coffee break.

Women still use the iron, of course, and occasionally men do too, although I doubt if any of them have ever ironed for four or five hours standing. But there are those who could tell you about that.

If you give this poem to the recreational director of a care center or retirement home today and have her read it to the silver-haired ladies and slipper-shuffling gentlemen who gather there on purple sofas, and then ask for their response, the sharing will be phenomenal.

I hated ironing … I loved ironing … I remember the starch we put in our clothes … I remember the little blue cube of wax we rubbed on the iron to make it slick … Yes, I remember that too and the lovely way it smelled … I remember the scent of clothes just in off the line after drying in the summer sun and breezes … I will never forget the way we dampened the dried clothes using a bottle with a sprinkler head and then rolled up the garments, placed them in a covered basket, and waited until they were uniformly damp … the hours I spent ironing in summer heat, the sweat dripping off the ends of my hair … Not me. We had an electric fan set on a chair and blowing directly on me, but of course then it dried out the damp shirt I was trying to iron.

Yes, the ladies will go on and on, and even the old codgers will chip in, remembering the feel of the carefully ironed shirt and the cool sheets smooth as silk. They will remember too that their mothers gripped a hot flatiron off the old wood-burning range and replaced it with another when it cooled.

And most of these wonderful old people, whose penmanship is good to this day, will have learned to write script by the Palmer Method. They will have stories about that too.

Palmer Method

I fall into a rhythm
With an iron in hand.
My arm, extension of my mind,
Does push-and-pulls and ovals
On the backs of shirts,
Signs cuffs and collars
With a flourish.
Shirttails almost meet
As one goes off and
One goes on the board,
So gracefully I work
Together with myself.
Thought roams free.
My fingers channel heat
To do the smoothing,
A laying on of hands
To discipline my pride
And touch my love
To wrinkled feelings
That need soothing.

The Family Hairlooms (And What to Do with Them)

I'm cleaning big time. Not just the usual dust and vac, but a real excursion into places long forgotten, where I've tucked things for sentimental reasons or because I might one day find a use for them. Now I'll be moving soon and need to be heartless in this search for things I no longer need.

I tackle the dresser. In the top drawer I find a small box and in it a lock of shiny, light brown hair tied with a pink ribbon. Enclosed is a note written by me in 1937. It reads: *Here is a lock of my hair. I am twelve years old.* Such a strange feeling, as I look up at my own silver hair in the mirror, to suddenly feel connected to that young girl I once was.

Then I find, rolled in barber's tissue, a lock of blonde hair that son number one brought home from his first butch haircut.

In another drawer I find an envelope with brown hair that son number two, at age three, sheared from his forehead the day before we were to have a family picture taken.

I know these fascinations with their own hair were normal, and it was normal also for them to have fascination, stage two, in their teens. But it was not normal for me to witness these stages without tearing my own hair.

Son number one was growing up when the Beatles hit, and he too wanted to play the guitar and sing and be cool like them. He did, in fact, play with a local band through his high school years. So, at graduation, we proudly watched him cross the stage, but not so proudly watched the bounce of his long, wavy locks. We were embarrassed over a trend we had never seen and could not manage.

Son number two walked the same stage ten years later. He had a nice head of hair but wore it short for sports. I mean really short for sports. Before graduation, to help him win the swim gold medal at state, he shaved not only his head but his entire body. Our only comfort on diploma day was the tasseled cap … until he threw it into the air.

I sit now on the bed's edge, daydreaming, trying to remember just when we all laughed and decided that hair was one thing we no longer needed to parent.

Now I tackle the deepest drawer, and there I find a rolled newspaper dated 1949. I open it, and out falls a long, shiny coil of beautiful, auburn hair, also tied with a pink ribbon.

Ah, I had forgotten where I put you, I think, *but I have not forgotten the day Grandma gave me the beautiful hair she had bobbed in 1926.*

Nor could I forget my daughter's blondish braids, which reached her waist before they were cut at age six. These I had finally mailed to her, along with her baptism dress and bonnet, with a note saying: *Now listen, there is a limit to how long you can store your stuff in my house.*

Sara with pigtails

One day she called me. "Mom," she said, "it's time for us to give up the hair, mine and your grandmother's."

She sent me online to research Locks of Love, Wigs for Kids, and other agencies that collect human hair to be made into wigs for children who have lost their hair while going through cancer treatment, or kids who have permanent loss because of disease.

A wonderful idea, I thought, and according to a website, our long locks might qualify even though my daughter was de-braided over fifty years ago, and my grandmother bobbed eighty-seven years ago. The hair was cut and stored properly and had been neither treated nor mistreated.

"So it's into a box with you, Grandma, and you'll be going on ahead as soon as we take care of details," I say, not realizing I'm making corny puns all over the bedroom. Yet I sense my grandmother Sarah and my daughter, Sara, laughing with me, loving the idea of sending their love on to children in such a way.

Now, to finish, I prepare two envelopes with a note to my sons:

> *My dears, here is your first haircut. You must know there is a limit to how long you can store your stuff in my house.*
>
> *Love, Mom*

Note: In 2014, my great-granddaughter Anna Markland sheared her beautiful, long locks and sent them to be used for other children.

Our American Idyll

It seems more than coincidence that the TV show *American Idol* claims our attention again just as election campaigns get going. Seen side by side, as they often are, these two wonders of television "entertainment" show a remarkable similarity. For instance:

1. In the beginning, a lot of people try out, and a surprising number make the grade for on-stage time. Colorful, yes, but when they perform in competition, the jokers are quickly spotted and laughed off the stage. Some home viewers skip this part, finding it silly, tuning in later when the competition narrows. But a lot of people, a really lotta people, get their kicks from watching the oddballs, the ones who dress funny and sing off-key. These viewers give up a few weeks into the fray and turn back to the comedy and sports channels without voting.
2. For the rest of us, the contest begins now. Week by week, as contestants move on toward the final segments, they come quickly under our close scrutiny. No allowance is made for one who forgets the words, has an off-key day, or screws up socially offstage. Their posture, their voice inflections, the look on their faces when performing and when not performing, even what they wear affects our impression. The camera takes us to their hometowns, and we see what kind of lives they lead and hear what they've done in the past.
3. Once the key performers are identified, certain changes begin to take place rather quickly, and we can guess that a lot of designer and rehearsal elves are at work backstage through the week to create instant transformation. The contestant's voice that once rose in harsh and frantic tones under pressure now sounds soft, controlled, measured … and folksy … friendly … familiar.

Hairstyles change overnight. Faces light up. Is it makeup, camera, or Botox?

4. After each performance, we listen to a panel of experts give their critiques. The experts are professionals, and they provide a show of their own. Now we're listening to the experts more than the performers. At the coffee shop, we are discussing with our friends which expert we would vote for.
5. We begin to cling to one or another final contestant. If one is voted out, we switch to another. It's only a game. We snack and drink our favorite drinks as we watch the show. We wonder if one will win because of the supporters they brought along with them or the ones they gained by their knockout performance and promise for the future. After all, the results hang on how many people voted, and we don't know who those people are. But we seldom bother to register our own opinion, and we are sometimes appalled by the results of the frequent polling. Are those voters crazy?
6. Finally, down to the line, we establish a firm favorite and are willing to support him/her to the finish. We may be more likely now to actually vote … but then again we may not. We assume everyone likes our candidate the best. We think he/she is a walk-away, so why bother.
7. Comes the big night. The final. We are so excited, those of us who rode it out. We might invite some friends in, have some snacks, some drinks. Waiting for the result is nerve-wracking, and we won't know the winner until the very last minutes of the show. And then it's over, and we're either surprised or not surprised, but it's over, and we can now go back to watching sports and game shows and soap operas. We say good-bye to our friends, the ones we didn't argue with, and tomorrow we'll say hello again to our friends on the other side who don't know sic'em about talent shows but aren't really bad people. If our choice lost, we'll remain very quiet, and if our side won, we'll remain quiet too, but we'll smile and wink at a true friend across the room, one who does know sic'em.

(Note to readers: Sic'em is perhaps a regional phrase, as in dog-trainer terms: "He don't know 'sic'em' from 'come here.'" In other regions, folks might say, "He don't know beans.")

The Mission

I knew a remarkable young lady from Tokyo. She married an American from our midlands, and one year she came here of her own free will to nurse her aged parents-in-law through one of our grueling, frigid winters. She arrived, a petite and stylish professional woman, donned an apron from her suitcase, and set about doing what she could to meet their needs and make them comfortable.

Early in the morning, I saw her out shoveling the sidewalks. Later she cleaned the house, cooked the meal, made their appointments, took them to the doctor, administered ointments, tucked them in.

Nothing she did was right. They misunderstood her motives from the beginning. Her cooking was strange, although she watched and memorized every move she had seen Mama make in the kitchen. If she talked, they thought her bossy. If she remained silent, they thought her aloof or conniving. Her very perfume offended them, clashed with their frugal atmosphere (and the smell of Vicks VapoRub). To top it off, they were German, from the old country, and staunch Lutherans. She was modern, Japanese, Buddhist, and liberated.

I asked Yasiko one day why she had undertaken such an impossible venture. "I believe that I have lived before and that I will live again," she said, "and while I am here, I must learn all I can. I am the youngest of three daughters in a culture where the oldest daughter bears the responsibility. The one thing I have been deprived of learning is the care and concern for the elderly or the sick. I come now to learn that."

It was not easy, and it grew more difficult. The winter was long and severe. The old folks griped and complained. They teased and insinuated she might have better things to do at home tending to her husband. Her husband, a former USA military officer and now a civil servant in military duties, was quite efficient. And Yasiko herself bore responsibilities there as hostess and social director for a well-known international hotel.

One day Yasiko came to my door, and I invited her in for tea. She sat and visited quietly about generalities, appreciating the opportunity to be away. She did not speak much of her situation, nor did I question. Yet, at the door, when she was ready to leave, tears welled up in her eyes. I put my arms out to her, and after one brave moment, she gave in, put her head on my shoulder, and wept her quiet tears of disappointment, of being misunderstood and unappreciated.

"Do not speak of this," she said. "I am ashamed to show such a weakness. I do not wish to fail in my mission. I will try harder, and I know that everything will be all right. You will see."

When winter played out and the last of the snow ran in trickles, when the sun shone fiercely and trees were budding, we went next door to pick up her bags and see Yasiko to the airport. She had been here five long months. The old folks lined up, and Mama, glad that she would have her house to herself once again and never unbending in her attitude, gave her brief thanks and what I thought was a token embrace … until I saw a tear glisten in her wizened eye.

Papa disappeared, and we found him in our car, prepared to accompany us to the airport. Once there, when the bags were checked, and the plane was in, Papa sat staring straight ahead. The flight was called. Gene and I hugged and wished Yasiko well. We started for the door. Then Papa moved. He shuffled toward Yasiko and put his arms out to her. "You are a good girl," he said. And then he hugged her, really hugged her, and I often wonder how many lifetimes he spared her.

And That Leaves Blue

I hadn't worked a jigsaw puzzle for years, but when my grandchildren gave me a gift of 750 little pieces of cardboard in a cardboard box with a stunning ocean scene on its cover, I knew they'd never let me rest until I put the thing together.

So we worked as a team at first, hovering around the card table, the kids and me … young, sharp eyes finding matches, little hands thrusting and crossing each other's as they placed their round-edged pieces into the border. It came together quickly, and when our holiday weekend was over, the picture was framed but empty. It would be round, as if it represented my world. And for a while it did. The children left, but I had made them a promise, and doing that puzzle was do or die.

The big picture, with its 750 components, was overwhelming, but the smaller pictures within it made the puzzle doable. I sorted pieces by color, setting aside all with orange tints for the giant lobster, gray ones for the whales, turquoise for the fish, browns for the mountain, pinks and greens for ocean vegetation. That left blue, and blue was everywhere.

I started slowly, minutes at a time. Then, tempted by every fish that needed just a fin or a bubble over his head, I began bringing my morning coffee to the puzzle table … and my afternoon tea.

I challenged myself to find at least five pieces before the buzzer went off from my clothes dryer or my oven. I stayed up a little later to finish a row of coral or a group of dolphins. By now, you might say, the fish had me hooked.

As with most things, the really fun part, the easy part, was early in the game, singling out and piecing together objects with bright colors, sharp lines. But then I graduated to seeking things less identifiable, like the stuff that grows on the ocean floor, the rows of tiny fish streaking about, the sunlight on a mountain slope, the foam on the crest of a wave.

Now I was sorting not just by color but by shades. Not just by shape but by idiosyncrasies of shape that in my frustration I started to name so I could find them and fit them into place where they belonged.

Many of the pieces looked like a body, with a head and limbs. But some had one arm or one leg, and I'd recognize a piece by the name of Lefty or Peg Leg. It was easy to recognize the shapes of clubs and spades, but the best clue was given by the "innies" and "outies." After all, they had to fit together. This helped, but seldom did I have a complete hole waiting to be filled. I'd be fitting one or two edges of a piece into the picture, or sometimes three (rarely four), so I needed a candidate that met at least one of the requirements.

At some point, the puzzle became less fun, more hard work. Some days I'd move pieces about aimlessly. Or I'd sit and stare at those little pictures, seeing no way to tie them into the big picture. Too many pieces, and they all began to look alike. It seemed I could not move into action until I chose one specific area, defined what it needed, and set my mind to look for nothing except what would fit there in that one small spot, even if it took me all afternoon.

Then it was *bingo*, whenever a piece fit. I knew it fit because it almost snapped into place. If I had to manipulate it to fit, it didn't. This was when I began to appreciate that the longer I worked intently on the hard spots, the bigger the bingo moment, the greater the incentive to go on with the puzzle.

The third phase came when I had completed everything but the background. The background was water and sky, lots of it. And that left blue. Every puzzle piece on my table was blue, and they all looked alike. Do you know how many shades of blue there are? (I looked it up online, and I got the answer "infinite.") Again I was forced to narrow my vision, set specific goals, and be led forward by the energy I gained from each small success.

Then one day the puzzle was finished. Sort of. There were no pieces left in the box, none on the table, none on the floor. But there were two glaring holes in the puzzle. I searched the area, searched the house … on hands and knees … with a flashlight. I didn't find the pieces. I smarted for a while but finally said, "Oh well, I did the best I could with what I had to work with. I'll put the puzzle away and keep it just in case." Wouldn't it be just like me to find the pieces months later, to find I had what it took, all the time, but had just dropped it, swept it under the rug?

Working a jigsaw puzzle is so much like doing any project. So much, in fact, like living a life. You learn as you go. You tackle the fun parts first and leave the drudgery to the end. Things that once looked impossible become possible. You go to bed early if you can't make a play, but you may stay up into the night after finding one wonderful key piece. *Success is addictive.*

PS—Later I did find the missing pieces. Guess where. Under the rug!

There is always someone who got a bigger puzzle than you did. (But that takes a lot more work.)

There are always those who have prettier puzzles than you do. (But look at them fifty years later!)

There are always people who have a very nice puzzle … but never open the box.

Touring in the Twenties

Jackson and Sarah Groves at Long Beach

My granddad Jackson Groves kept a diary all his life, but the one that came down to me was from 1926, the year he and my Grandma Sarah drove their Hudson from the middle of Iowa to Long Beach, California. Can you imagine what a trip that was?

They were fifty-seven that year, retired and moved into town, where he was eventually their long-time mayor. As far as I know, neither of them had ever been out of Iowa, so every page of the diary reflects their awesome first view of red dirt … cotton fields … mountains … oil derricks … cactus … orange trees … ocean.

They rose early in Stanhope, Iowa, to a raw cloudy day on November 16, and Granddad sat down to write in his journal: "We are starting on a trip we have often dreamed of but hardly hoped to take. Will we be disappointed or surprised? Let this little book tell as we go along."

They climbed into their Hudson and drove to Webster City, where they met friends who would be traveling in tandem with them, and were on their way by nine o'clock, driving on dirt roads. Across Iowa they struggled with muddy ruts that forced them to travel at 15 mph all the way to Omaha. There they checked into a hotel, and in the morning they were pleased to be on gravel roads for a while. By evening, they were all the way through Kansas and into Oklahoma. They had eight more days of driving ahead of them and were pleased that the red dirt of Oklahoma made for good roads.

In Texas they found themselves on concrete pavement for 175 miles but were soon bumping around on dirt roads again, sometimes getting stuck or sliding off the road. It is not mentioned in his diary, but I remember my mother telling that Granddad put several logs in the car, and he would chain them to the bumper to slow his descent down steep mountains.

They sometimes stopped to visit with locals, particularly farmers, and at dusk they found a hotel for the night in Texas (three times), Arizona, and California. All stops were carefully documented with the name of the hotel and a record of the costs for the day, including gas, food, and hotel. No day exceeded $5.32, and some days cost no more than three dollars.

They arrived in Long Beach in the rain, which dimmed their first view of the ocean but not of luscious flowers and orchards of fruit. They were pleased to secure a very suitable apartment for thirty-five dollars per month, including everything necessary, for this would be their home for almost five months. After quickly settling in, they strolled to the pier for a free band concert and bought oysters to prepare for their supper. I can imagine how good it must have felt to stretch their legs and to smell the fresh scent of the open water.

There were lots of Iowans visiting as they were, and many of these Iowans had relatives and old friends living in California as well, the Iowa migration having brought an estimated 160,000 Iowans to the coast from 1918 to 1930. And so from the time of their arrival, there were surprise visitors at the door, and also many reasons to go for long ocean-view drives to seek out other Iowans, with stops along the way to picnic, to marvel at scenic valleys, rugged coastlines, and acres of brilliant orange groves.

In the mornings, the housewives did their housework. Afternoons they strolled the streets, shopping for postcards and needlework, or took in a matinee. One day Granddad wrote that Mrs. Groves had walked downtown to have her hair "amputated." (This was the year the ladies had their long hair bobbed.)

The men joined a club where they went to play checkers and horseshoes. Evenings the couples invited guests for dinner or were invited out for dinner, after which they played a card game called Five Hundred. There were afternoons at the beach for all and day trips by auto to Los Angeles, Huntington Beach, Laguna Beach, San Pedro, Santa Monica, Glendale, Santa Anna, Pomona. Many times they swam and combed Redondo Beach for moonstones, which the ladies had polished and made into rings.

Sometimes they ate out, and Granddad wrote they were thrilled to find "a place where you sat down at a revolving table and helped yourself to whatever and as much as you wanted for the price of 45 cents." They went to museums and musicals. They walked down to the pier where they toured the battleship *Colorado* (over five hundred feet long!) and also saw the *New Mexico*, *West Virginia*, *Arizona*, *Tennessee*, and other great ships of the US fleet.

Of course they took a boat to Catalina Island, after which Granddad wrote that they were both sick, coming and going, and that he had given up all plans of becoming a pirate. Another day they were guests of a land lot company on a boat ride around the harbor, a trip to the lots for dinner, and then the sales pitch (has nothing changed?). The lots were 45 x 140 and were priced to them at $2,100.

On January 1, 1927, Granddad wrote: "Well, we have seen the great Tournament of Roses at Pasadena. Most beautiful. Eighty-eight floats with millions of roses and flowers decorating them, 28 bands, horsemen and foot marchers galore. They said 750,000 people were there and the parade was miles long. Took one hour, twenty minutes, to pass. Saw Hoot Gibson in the parade. Never saw such a crowd in my life, and the traffic jam was fierce."

Friends who lived in Beverly Hills took them for a personal tour in their Buick. Granddad wrote: "This is the most beautiful district we've seen. Saw most of the movie folks' estates, which were on a lavish scale …

Harold Lloyd, Chaplin, Valentino, Fairbanks, Mix, Theda Bara, Norma Talmidge, Gloria Swanson, Mary Pickford, Poli Negri, and others."

On February 26, they went to the famous annual Iowa Picnic, and he wrote: "Big crowd. Not much going on but visiting. Met old friends, some not seen for 25 years."

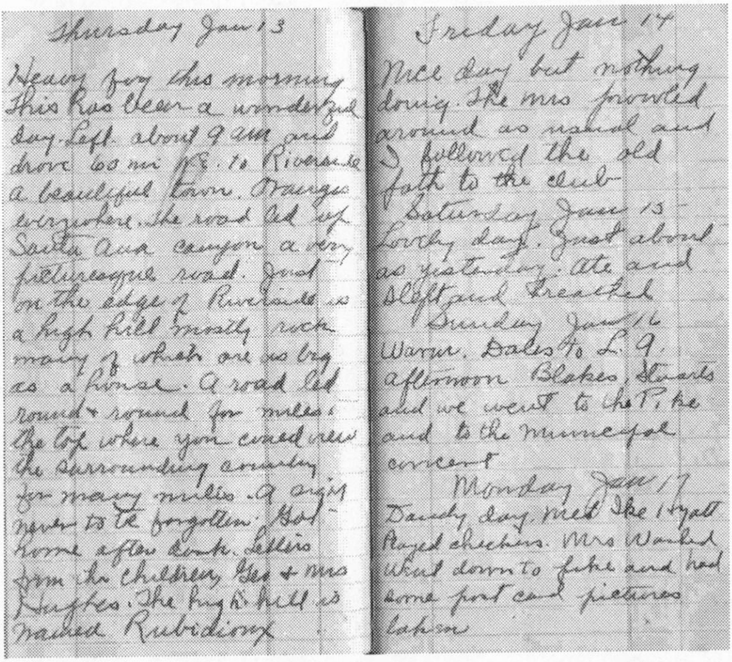
Thursday Jan 13
Heavy fog this morning
This has been a wonderful
day. Left about 9 am and
drove 60 mi E. to Riverside
a beautiful town. Oranges
everywhere. The road led up
Santa Ana canyon a very
picturesque road. Just
on the edge of Riverside is
a high hill mostly rock
many of which are as big
as a house. A road led
round & round for miles to
the top where you could view
the surrounding country
for many miles. A sight
never to be forgotten. Got
home after dark. Letters
from the children, Geo & Mrs
Hughes. The high hill is
named Rubidioux

Friday Jan 14
Nice day but nothing
doing. The mrs prowled
around as usual and
I followed the old
path to the club
Saturday Jan 15
Lovely day. Just about
as yesterday. Ate and
slept and breathed
Sunday Jan 16
Warm. Dales to L. B.
afternoon Blakes, Stuarts
and we went to the Pike
and to the Municipal
concert
Monday Jan 17
Dandy day. Met Ike Hyatt
Played checkers. Mrs Ward
went down to Pike and had
some post card pictures
taken

They visited many churches but were most impressed at the Angelus Temple where they heard Aimee Semple McPherson, the popular evangelist of that day. Granddad wrote: "The Temple is a fine edifice seating 5000 people and was filled. Mrs. McPherson is a remarkable woman. She preached and baptized 108 people, many claiming to have been healed by prayer of diseases called almost incurable."

There is no question that winter was the most marvelous winter of their lives, and yet on March 17, Granddad wrote: "I'm getting tired of California and am ready to go home." Another day, in a cynical moment, he wrote: "The ravens brought us half a blueberry pie, so the day was not entirely wasted."

They left March 31, as planned, and their return route took them through a petrified forest, a painted desert, Albuquerque, Las Vegas, and

Colorado Springs. Like its master, the Hudson had tired. On April 6, Granddad wrote: "We left Fort Morgan (Co) at 7:00 a.m. Satan left about the same time, as we had three down tires and got nine miles off the road." And on the last two days, they had a blowout and two more flat tires … in the rain.

They arrived home, live and well, on April 8, 1927. Granddad wrote on the last page of his journal: "And so ends our trip. Wonderful in so many ways and never to be forgotten. Old friends look best and home the best. The entire trip cost about $565."

The Nest Is Never Empty
... Till You Leave It

Part I—The Elephant in the Room

Late in life, one would think, you are over the hurdles. Let's see, the kids are raised and gone, the rat race ended, and a pension check comes every month to help pay the bills. Now there is time for travel, for reflection, for hobbies, for good works, good books, good friends, and long dinner conversations. There is time to invite the grandchildren (or even the great-grandchildren) for afternoons, overnights, or extended stays. Frankly, one couldn't have a better life.

So why do I worry? Well, it's a mother's nature to worry, and even after she sees that her middle-aged children are doing well and their children are doing well, there are still things to worry about.

Top of the list is this house. I never thought of it as empty when we found ourselves alone here, not only because it's so full of memories but because the children left so much of their stuff here. It has taken years of cajoling and finally eBay to clear it out, right down to the seventies flare jeans, rock band posters, ice skates, and forty-fives.

Still the rooms are full of furniture, the closets full of clothes, the basement storeroom full of everything we ever bought and used and stored to use again. And the market keeps tempting us with new gadgets to buy and use and store to use again. Living takes a lot of stuff, but our imaginations acquire even more.

What are we going to do with it all when we must leave? I constantly assess my need, pausing now and then to ask, "Will I have a use for this in a smaller place or (gulp) in a nursing home?" And one by one, I let a few pieces go at my garage sales. But still the rooms are full of furniture, the closets full of clothes, and the storeroom keeps on storing.

When our grown children, and even our grown grandchildren, come for visits, we have a wonderful time, and they fit right back in. But I notice how they roam the house, breathing in its ambiance and placing their memories. And when they prepare to leave, the car packed and running, how they step back in to search for something they forgot and make a final walk-through, returning with a tissue in hand.

But we don't talk about it. The elephant in the room is the room itself and all the space around it. How much longer can we keep it, and what do we do then?

I've been where my children are now. I remember the nostalgia of my last visits, driving over the river and through the woods to the home place in Iowa where I grew up, and that sentimental last look back as we drove down the country lane on our way back to the city.

After Dad died, my mother stayed on there for a few years but finally sold the farm and bought a sweet, little cottage on a lake in the Ozarks where she could pursue her hobbies and be near my brother. It was a terrible shock, losing my original home base, and it was hard on my children because this was Grandma and Granddad's house. But we survived. Mom's later moves to a town house, then an apartment, then assisted living did not bother me at all. Those places were good for her, and they had never been nests to me.

Maybe, when the time comes and my age is as golden as my mother's was, the decision will be taken out of my hands, and with a little push I will leave this nest as gracefully as I left the first one we ever owned.

Part II—Moving On

In 1963, we sold our first home and moved from one small city in the Midwest to another small city in the Midwest, a distance of less than two hundred miles on the map but a distance of thousands of miles in my mind. My husband left a very secure job with a large corporation to take on a much bigger job with a small company. It meant moving further instate, away from the major shopping centers, the major airports, and most of all, away from my routines, away from my friends.

At that time of life, my friends were those whose husbands worked with my husband and whose babies were born when my babies were born. At bridge club, we compared walking, talking, and teething stories, chicken pox symptoms, and recipes. Summer afternoons we gathered around the community pool and taught the children how to swim. Winter weekends we gave dinner parties and danced the new years in.

The change in plans came as a sudden shock to me and at a bad time. I was in another state, in a hospital wing sitting with my dying father when the phone call came informing me that the decision had been made and real estate strangers were already combing my house for selling points. Strangers in my house! I could not imagine, and still cannot imagine, anything more likely to fill me with actual panic.

But it was done, and when set into motion, all things come to pass. My father died. My house was sold. We packed our belongings and all the precious things we had accumulated, necessities really because our tastes were simple and our income limited. In the last few days, I worked almost around the clock, obsessed with something that seems to be a part of me, the thought that I must never leave a place worse than I found it … in fact, if possible, to leave it in better condition.

So, as I cleared each room, I scrubbed and polished. I sanded the windowsills and applied a fresh coat of varnish. I sterilized the bathroom and the kitchen, waxed the floors and buffed them with an electric polishing machine. When I closed the doors on the empty linen closet, I left there a map showing the layout of the flower garden, an X marking the spot of each bulb that would surprise the new owners with tulips, grape hyacinths, and gladioli in the spring.

My husband had gone on ahead with our son John on the final day, and my daughter, Sara, and I stayed behind to close the house. By now it was empty, beautiful, promising, the rooms echoing with our memories while beckoning for others to supplant them. Even as I took that last walk-through, I knew I did not belong there. Already I was an impostor in another's space.

I sent Sara to the car and spent a moment alone in this, our first nest. Instinctively I closed my eyes and just enjoyed once more the feelings we'd known in this happy place. When I walked out the door, I took our personal energy with me, freeing the space for others to find their happiness there.

Back in the car, a tissue in hand, I turned the key and drove toward the setting sun, headfirst into the unknown. That's the way it's done. It's called "moving on." So I've done it before, and when the time is right, I will do it again.

(Note: I did do it again in much the same way, in 2013, two years after my husband's death. I worked very hard to leave that big family home like a new home to its new owners, and in the process, I "copied" and filed away my memories, taking them along to store in a safe place in my beautiful but much smaller new home.)

Articles I Started

and then decided
one paragraph
probably said
it all

When I was a small child, I knew more than I know now in many ways. I had no doubts about anything. What I was, I just was. What I did, I just did. No one could ask me anything that I couldn't answer with something. I always knew where I was going and what I wanted to do. I loved everyone. I would do anything for them.

* * * * * *

Statistics back up the fact that the expiration date, or the deadline, for men often comes earlier that their mate's. Anyone who has ever lived in a normal family situation can understand this very well. Of course. The men go first. As always, the women stay behind to clean up.

* * * * * *

Politics has become the great divider. Some people actually hate those who don't see things the way they do. So silly. So wrong. Have you ever moved to a different city and gone through the process of fitting in with a new circle of friends? And then you find that you all have similar views and are aligned with the same political party? There were other nice people in the community, but theirs was a different vibration. There really are two or more ways of seeing the world with its complicated structures, and we can be thankful. It takes two to tango. It takes two animals to pull a heavy load. It takes two of anything to form a family. It takes two philosophies, or more, to keep a balance in the government. We know what happens when there is only one.

Living Moments

Listen to the House

I listen to the house in the morning
when the energy has not been stirred
but hangs in sleepy pockets of each room,
revitalized, ready to be unzipped
and opened for the day.

I listen to the house again at night
when everyone has gone to bed.
It creaks in spots, as timbers shift,
as wind gusts tickle air vents.
The rooms are full, packed with shadows
of our busy-ness, of joy we've shared,
with echoes of the words we've said,
the feelings left unsaid.

Lightly they will settle, dust to dust,
these words and feelings of the earth,
as all of us lie down in perfect trust
and drift into the universe to rest.

Sun Bonnet Sue

My life was planned
and carefully pieced
by loving hands and the
wisdom of the elders.
Pampered from the
moment of my birth,
I had the best room
in the house, always,
and folks exclaimed
my beauty.

I've never traveled
or thought of any life
beyond that peaceful room
on the west where the
sun falls on me in the afternoon
and sudden breezes move the shades,
where guests are shown
just to look at me or to
gather comfort for the night.

So now, can you imagine
me perched on an old
card table in the garage …
the garage!
It's hot in here, and
people touch me …
they *touch me*
and comment not upon
my beauty but to say
I'm frayed around the edges.

Who is not a bit frayed
when they are old?

Who has not changed their shape
or felt some stuffing shift?

I watch the faces, feel the hands,
and dread the ones who want
to throw me into musty campers
or cut me up for rags.
At best I'll grab the mother's heart
of a creative one who'll mold me
into teddy bears and rabbits,
loving the novelty of my patina,
the feel of memories and
grandma love for all
her little girls.

Yes, I'll go with that.

The Horizon

Always, always the horizon is there,
Never changing except for a sunrise,
A sunset, or a car going over the hill.
When I turn, I face another like it,
And the only difference is the light coming up
Or the light going down, and both have
A beauty that takes my breath away.
Always I have lived within this frame,
Safe, knowing I could wander
And never fall over the edge,
Never disappear from my world
And the world of those I love.
How could I think that time would
Change the order of things
And the world would stop
When my step slowed
And the horizon seemed far away.
It is supposed to be far away.
I can never reach it.

Walls

I tried to reach you once.
We were alone,
And it was late.
I told you things
I'd never mentioned
In the daylight,
Dreams and visions
That came true,
Feelings, knowings,
Inner stirrings
That I knew
To be inspired.

You yawned and said,
"Another time …
Tonight I am so tired."

Hang Loose

The tour guide had us laughing
From the time he met our flight.
In the bus and in the lobbies,
On the moonlit beach at night,
He cast a spell.
"Hang loose," he said,
And island magic
Helped us do it well.

"Hang loose," he said,
"For life is short,
And while you are away,
Relearn the art,
A time for work
And now a time for play."

"Hang loose," he said,
And taught us how
To sign it with our thumbs,
And, laughing, no one saw when he
Took twenty seconds privately
To ask me for a Tums.

Living Memories

The Round Table

Back on the farm in Iowa,
Our chalice was the coffee cup,
And every day at ten and four,
The pot was perked to fill it up.

Then freshly frosted cakes were cut,
And summer's jams and jellies spread,
Without a thought of calories,
On yeasty loaves of good, warm bread.

True feelings passed with perfect ease,
Along with chunks of longhorn cheese,
And tension melted into cheer
With Arthur there, with Guinevere
And any knight who happened by
And smelled the cinnamon of pie.

When winter ringed us in with snow,
When harvest days were cruel and hot,
We stopped our work at ten and four
To gather 'round the coffee pot,
To eat, to talk, and laugh a lot
In harmony, our Camelot.

Snow Vacation

I remember mornings
When the windowpanes were white
With snow that fell and frosted
Into crystals overnight,
And mother calling up the stairs,
"There'll be no school today!"
And then the rush to all decide
What we should do … and play.

First, I'm sure, there were some chores,
And then began the fun.
Rook was great, and Authors too,
But when those games were won,
We set up for Monopoly,
A game we loved to play,
And it's well named because it did
Monopolize our day.

We popped some corn,
And as we munched,
The scent began to rise
Of peanut butter fudge our Mom
Had cooked for a surprise.
Oh what carefree hours we spent
Because we didn't know
When we grew up we'd be the ones
To shovel all the snow.

The Quilting Bee

An afternoon at Grandma's
Was always fun for me,
Especially when ladies came
For Grandma's quilting bee.
They let me thread a needle,
Although, without a doubt,
My long and crooked stitches
Were later taken out.

When I was tired of sewing,
The quilt became my tent.
From underneath I watched to see
Where all those stitches went.
Butterflies and bonnets,
Garden paths and pointy stars
Would grace the cozy quilts
The ladies made for church bazaars.

But best of all, I liked it
When quilters took a break
With cups of tea or coffee
And Grandma's angel cake.
I also loved their promise
(Which later did come true):
"When you grow up and marry, dear,
We'll quilt a quilt for you."

LEARNING

Young and Old

The Testy Two-Year-Old

The two-year-old in overalls,
With Band-Aids and with bruises,
Who can know how hard he works,
What energy he uses.
Up and down and in and out
From one place to another
He pulls his toys, to keep within
The aura of his mother.
He turns the faucet, pokes the cat,
Shoves tinker toys in places,
Falls off his trike, invents a hike
To look for friendly faces.
Give him room, the two-year-old
In jelly and pajamas;
He only learns by testing
Faucets, cats, and folks and grandmas.

Great Grandma

She keeps her peace
and watches
from the sidelines
all the others
doing what she did
when she was star,
when she was coach,
when she was coach's coach.

Sometimes she sees
the play that's needed,
cheers, no matter
what they choose,
posts their wins on fridges
and empathizes sadly
when they lose.

But Grandma shuts
her mouth and shuts
her eyes from time to time,
to hold a little conference
with the players, in her mind.

Thoughts on Life

My Comings and Goings

I tend to wade into life
The way I wade into water …
First testing with my toes,
Then standing in the sand
To feel the water flow
Until it draws me slowly in,
Two shivers to my ankle,
Six shivers to my knee,
With long waits between steps
When the strong waves slap
And swirl around my tender thighs.
I always dive … eventually …
And once I do, I'm warm and
So at peace I can't imagine
Why I didn't leap at once into
What feels like home.

Wading out is easier.
There is no shock in going back
To where I've walked before.
Gently guiding with my arms
And swishing with my feet,
I ride the waves toward shore
Until I feel the shelf of sand.
I stand and wave to friends
And loved ones on the beach
Who motion "come and join us
In the sun again," and offer towels
And arms to warm and welcome me.

Centering

I love a breather in an airport,
Floating free, with hours to wait,
Gliding by on ramps with other torsos,
Queuing up with other legs
For confirmation at the gate,
Sitting down on smooth and rounded plastic,
Smiling when I meet another smile,
Trusting, for the stranger with a ticket,
Knowing where he's going,
On his way, confirmed,
Is free from guile.

Rooms for contemplation on the concourse
Fill with busy, busy people pulled aside,
Stopped from all their comings and their goings,
Bodies placed on hold while hearts and minds confide.

I have rapport with passengers in limbo,
Sorting out their heavens and their hells,
Touching down to reach their earthy feelings,
Taking off when destiny impels.

Weaving

There's a slender thread of silence
On the silken edge of sleep
When the sun goes down
On the day I've made
And the memories I'll keep.
It's a very private moment,
Meant for sorting and review,
When the wisdom from the lessons
I've been learning filters through
To my surprise …
And for a fraction of a second,
I am wise.
Then I find myself in a nether world
Of fantasy and dreams
Where life as viewed from the underside
Is seldom what it seems,
But through a mirror darkly
All my wants, my doubts, and fears
Take on form, with names and faces
Going back throughout the years
To help me find …
The perfect pattern for the life
I had in mind.
At dawn I reach the threshold
Of a quiet, hidden church,
Knock, and enter with the password
Of the honest soul in search,
Know the peace and silent blessing
That were always within reach
But withheld until the dawning
When my greater self could teach
My longing soul …
And for a fraction of a second,
I am whole.

Seesaw

How great a balance friendship strikes
When two or more can share.
For always one is on the ground,
And one is in the air.
Our ups and downs can even out
When others shift the weight
And hold us by their faith
Until we grasp our fickle fate
And count it sweet,
Pushing up from solid ground again
On sturdy feet.

Twenty-Five Words or Less

Two billboards grabbed my attention as I drove across town. One listed Wednesday's lottery drawing for $240 million. The other promoted the movie *The Prize Winner of Defiance, Ohio* in which Julianne Moore played the part of a housewife in the fifties who supported her family by writing winning jingles or statements of the "why I like your product in twenty-five words or less" variety.

Hey! Been there, done that, I thought. No, I didn't support my family, but I brought a little excitement into the home now and then when I won a prize in just such a contest. These were entirely different from promotions and games today, which are basically drawings, and in which I have no interest, no luck, even if I choose for my numbers the kids' birthdays or the numbers on my fortune cookie.

But, ah, the creative contest, that is something in which I once had a healthy interest and that made my heart race in a very good way. No giveaway, that. You sang for your supper. In the fifties and into the sixties, my songs were words scribbled on every notepad in the house, on the backs of envelopes, and running constantly across the bottom of my mental screen. As soon as a new contest was announced, I started using the sponsor's product to discover what made it unique and to write descriptive words that would set my entry apart from hundreds of thousands, sometimes millions of other entries.

Not many prizes were offered, so when I saw how few entries were to be chosen, I realized that the odds of my winning were not great. Then it occurred to me, "If you can't lick 'em, join 'em," and at the library I found books and articles on how to write for contests. That is, how to say a lot in a brief space by drawing word pictures and using wordplay and other techniques to project meaning clearly and colorfully. I learned it was equally important to just be myself and be honest, that prizes could be won by very ordinary people with good product discernment.

There were no million-dollar prizes then. Top prize was often a trip, an automobile, furniture, appliances, jewelry, or cash in amounts of a few thousand dollars. The most popular contests asked you to write a jingle about a product or write a statement of a specified type in twenty-five words or less. Deadlines were tight, and at most you would have a few weeks to compose and send your entry. Sometimes I ran across a contest ad that I'd missed earlier, and so I had only a few days, or even hours, to put my thoughts together and squeeze and polish them into something this side of brilliant.

I had always loved words, but I tended to be wordy, so those around me would agree, I'm sure, that one thing I needed was practice in being concise. Now I also became an observer, testing products and jotting in my notebook my sincere opinions. My rug rats became laboratory rats, as I used them to test soaps and cereals and underwear. We played free association games, and I made lists of words, ideas, and feelings, experimenting with puns or other devices that would give two meanings for the price of one or create leaps of thought without explanation.

Then I worked, not with my mind but with my elbows and my knees. Armed with my endless lists, the subconscious was assigned to work on its own for hours while I scrubbed floors, weeded the garden, baked bread, ironed clothes, painted the ceiling. The inspiration came, always, as I turned the shirt, stirred the soup, stroked the brush, or rocked the baby, when my conscious mind was well out of the way and I was most relaxed. That's the way the unconscious works, providing you have given it something to work with.

Not content to put all my eggs in one basket, I usually sent more than one entry per contest, which was just fine with the sponsor because he had asked for a product label with each entry, and the purpose of the contest in the first place was to sell more product.

I remember times when I worked on five to ten contests at once, so it was necessary to keep a project board and to set specific goals with deadlines. When all my entries were in the mail, I moved that contest off the board and forgot about it, because I had done my 50 percent and was eager to get on with the next challenge. (The other 50 percent, you ask? My muse, of course.)

Entries were screened over a period of weeks by an independent judging agency, which employed panels of judges to read and score entries, narrowing them down to a final judging. They were meticulously scored on such criteria as content, originality, clarity, and conciseness. Small-prize winners, once determined, were notified by mail; major-prize winners received phone calls, telegrams, or personal calls before delivery of the prize.

There were disappointments when I lost but never time to dwell on it, since I had other entries in the mail. There were celebrations when I won, and here are some of the prizes that came by special delivery: bicycles and various unusual, large toys for my children, radios, a blender, an electric mixer, an electric knife, a silver coffee and tea service, a complete stereo system with beautiful wood cabinet, a Thomas organ, a ring with a large star sapphire surrounded by twenty-one diamonds, a Philco portable TV, various amounts of money … and, finally, the biggest prize I had ever won.

Such a day that was. The phone rang. A man introduced himself and asked if I would be home at a certain time. I knew this meant a prize was coming, and I wasn't surprised, because weeks before I had been checked out by a Pinkerton detective agent who drove up from Kansas City to interview me. (Had I written the entry by myself? Was I an employee or were any of my relatives employees of the sponsor? Etc.) The agent told me that my entry had reached the top and would place either first or second in the final judging. That was heady stuff, considering that this was a huge national contest, first prize was ten thousand dollars (a lot of money in those days), and second prize was a baby blue station wagon. But then you must realize that the Rambler station wagon sold then for $2,600.

So now you know why I was not jumping up and down when I realized that the phone call came from my local automobile agency. Well, let's be honest. Money is better. Add to that the fact that I had just washed my hair, and now I'm told that a representative from the Quaker Oats Company in Chicago would be at my house within minutes along with the car dealer, a photographer, and a reporter.

That night the local newspaper carried a large picture of the station wagon, with my kids sitting on top, waving their little arms off, and me standing alongside with dripping wet hair and wishing I were anywhere else. But I was smiling, because my part of the bargain was to give the sponsor more good advertising, and because I really was happy after all that I had won a fine prize.

If you want to be a winner in this type of contest, you do your part. Luck enters in, of course. People told me I was lucky, and, although I had worked very hard on my entries, I said to them, "Yes, I really am lucky," because it seemed to make them feel better, but also because I knew I was lucky.

I was lucky that I had a feeling for words. I was also lucky because as a housewife in those days, I was home all day and had the time to refine my ideas and get them to the post office. Prizes are not won by people with good intentions but by people whose entries are in the mail, preferably more than one. I was lucky to be born into a family with attitudes of persistence (do or die but never give up!). I may have been lucky that a judge somewhere in New York City got up on the right side of the bed, or had a good breakfast, or had a sense of humor like mine.

My favorite prize of all was the 1959 Philco Safari television, because it was a top prize, was the very first portable television to come out, and because it was delivered to my door during a fierce snowstorm on Christmas Eve, and the kids went wild! It was beautiful. It was all bright gold brass and golden brown leather. It had a leather handle, and the body was easily tilted.

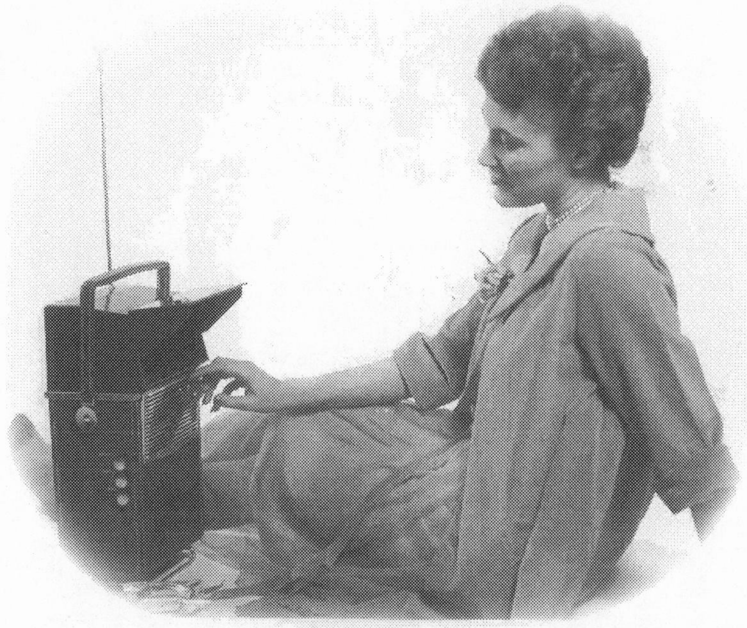

My sister admires my prize

That little Safari did in fact go on safaris with us, so to speak ... summer vacations and trips to Grandma's. It was my bedside companion as well and went with me for hospital stays. Sometime in the nineties, I sold that darling Safari, still in perfect condition, on a private online auction, and I'm told that it is now on display in the number-one spot in the window of a TV museum in London. So while you might say I never actually won a trip, one of my prizes won a trip!

I sold the station wagon and with the proceeds took my husband and two children on the Silver Bullet scenic train from the Midwest to Los Angeles, and then a coastal train to San Francisco. What a wonderful time we had, and, believe me, they deserved it.

I missed those fun contests when they were replaced by coupons for random drawings. I think the drawings were too random for me, but then, come to think of it, I don't believe I ever entered one. Drawings don't draw my attention. They just don't set my ticker ticking and my mind clicking.

I would like to see sponsors take us back again to that period of creative fun, when magazines came every month with details and entry blanks for contests with exotic prizes. Maybe we should write and tell them so, in twenty-five words or less.

I Heart My IBM Computer

I've become so used to my computer with all its uses that I have forgotten what a frightening challenge it was when I bought my first one in the early nineties. Recently I found a few things I had scribbled about those awesome few days.

* * * * * *

I have owned a computer now for four days and all the while have been thinking I must make note of what I am experiencing. To buy a computer is to enter into a new world, and since I bought and installed this IBM home model on a Saturday, I had first to experience a "lost weekend" before I could begin to gather my thoughts.

Entering the computer world must be akin to entering the physical world. I am here, fresh and new to the scene, eager to learn, and because it's very complicated, I tire easily. A few hours of computer hunt and peck on Saturday afternoon, and I have to be put down for a nap, with a throbbing headache.

Sunday morning I skip my usual brunch-with-crossword breakfast and any kind of formal devotion to devote my attention instead to the lessons that I discover are programmed into my hard drive. Interesting, isn't it, that I'll be dealing in software and hard drive. I'll think about that later. Words carry subtle meanings, and there are no mistakes.

Built into my computer is a word processor with a terrific menu. I love that word "menu" because it suggests choices and also because a menu of word choices has always excited me more than a menu of food choices. Imagine being able to push buttons and have words spring to life and then to discover that you can move them around, enlarge them, design the style of them, draw pictures or space around them, copy them on paper, file them away for later use … or cursor and destroy them.

So I set about learning how to do all of the above at once, so eager to learn that I wander in and out of options and choices and find myself lost in a maze time and time again. "How did I get here?" and "How do I get back to where I was?" and "Where do I go from here?"

Every few hours I drag myself to the kitchen for food and water (or aspirin), and this orientation orgy continues through Sunday morning, afternoon, evening, and into the night.

Some of the more obvious lessons of life that the computer taught me in these initial sessions were these: 1) Everything I need to know is already built in. I just need to learn how to get to it. 2) You can't make a mistake. No matter what buttons I push, I am going to learn something. 3) If I get lost, the Escape button takes me back at least one step so I can catch my breath. There are lots of other options. It takes patience to discover them. 4) When I'm in trouble and all else fails, I can just turn everything off for a while.

I did this a couple of times, and it gave me the emptiest feeling, as if all my efforts had been in vain and I had nothing in my hand to take with me. After that, I got out the manuals and studied hard, not to save face but to enlarge my potential and understand my choices, determined while in a strange land to take some notes and grab some maps and souvenirs so I'll know my way around next time I come back.

I thought about that and wondered how many people in life get themselves caught in a maze of human instruction, sidetracked and frightened, and simply turn off the set. I want to say to them, "Wait! There is always a way. Wait! Let's get out the index and look up O for options or C for commands or S for search."

The World Is My Cloister

I was earlier than some in my age group to take up the computer, so word got out around town that I was very good at it. I asked a friend why anyone should think so, and she said it was because I spent so much time on the thing. Somehow it never occurred to my friends and neighbors that I spent a lot of time at the computer because I was *not* very good at it.

But then, early computers did require more patience and skill than most of us had, and while I taught myself (slowly) how to put my ideas into files and to organize them and then find them again, without getting lost myself, I never did come to understand DOS.

I still have that first tiny but bulky computer in my basement, and I've hung on to it as I've hung on to memories of my childhood and my first love.

In 1995, I updated to a snazzy desktop, now much simplified, and within hours I was online. When I made that first connection to the web, it truly was an electric one. That's when a whole new world opened for me.

Almost instantly I was e-mailing family and long lost friends, reading the news, researching whatever I happened to wonder about, and playing my way through Solitaire, Tetris, Bookworm, and any other game that did not require a partner. Now I was spending time on the computer because it was fascinating and much more fun than doing dishes.

I was puzzled by my friends who did not get computers and join in the fun. I was just as puzzled by people who bought computers and never used them.

I knew a very nice lady who bought a computer and put it in an upstairs bedroom, where she went occasionally to play a game of solitaire. When guests came, she took them upstairs and opened the door so they could look in and admire her computer. It was a year or more before she sent her first e-mail.

Well into this century, I have abandoned my fourth desktop and am using only my laptop, since my lap goes everywhere I go. I've located fellow graduates, traced my genealogy back to terribly important Irishmen and a few Swedish farmers, managed my investments, and kept in touch with all my living relatives but especially my kids.

When the youngest one was in and out of Afghanistan and Iraq for five years, I relied on his e-mails to know he had safely flown his big plane across that ocean and to know, day to day, that he was all right. His e-mails, when he could make them, took me into his world and let me live it with him for the moment and let me sleep at night.

With lots of help from the Internet, I've dreamed, typed, mailed, and sold a few of my precious ideas that had lain at the bottom of my brain through all the years that I raised those kids and cleaned that house and cooked those meals.

When an observant grandson noticed his grandfather watching TV alone in the family room while I was back in my office on the computer, he brought me a modem so I could use my laptop anywhere in the house.

Now in the evenings I can be in my comfortable chair answering mail, sorting pictures, making notes, bidding on eBay, posting to my favorite list group, researching prices, or making reservations while all the time watching TV with one eye. I can do two things at once because I am a woman. (When my husband watches TV, he watches TV.)

But the programs raise so many questions that every once in a while he signals me and says, "Hey, look this up, would you?" Things like: Is Kirk Douglas still alive? What's the weather for next week up in Minnesota? Oh, what's the name of that guy that used to be Barney Fife? Just where is Uzbekistan? *Click, click*, and he has his answer. Better yet, I pull up Google Earth and take him there.

For a moment, he has stepped into my world … the world of facts, ideas, pictures, places, people, opportunity, convenience, communication, and comfort.

So now, you see, whether I'm traveling, lounging in my leather chair, or riveted to my office chair, I have one hand on the mouse not because I'm addicted but because I've found so many places to go without moving a muscle except the ones in my fingers. Who could ask for more?

Connecting

My family wonders why I am so fascinated
with my computer, and perhaps they think
I go to weird or foolish sites
to spend my time, to get away.
Why else would I disappear for hours
and be lost to them? How could they know?

In the thirties, times were tough,
and money was scarce.
A quiet child with few toys,
I amused myself with dreams.
A cardboard box, punched with holes,
became a switchboard. With
string attached, I pushed a pencil
in and out, wearing earmuffs for my headset,
voicing, "Number, please. I will connect you."

I talked my mother out of an old table,
small but interesting, a rose embossed
on the surface, the varnish cracking now
but still smooth to the touch, and here
I set up office hours, taking notes and
planning, writing letters, writing poems,
organizing what I thought of
on the little scraps I had.

But there was never paper.
I asked for paper, and my mother
gave me paper, one sheet of paper.
I wanted reams of paper.
I had reams of ideas.
And I wanted to connect with people!
I wanted to know what they looked like,
I wanted to know what they thought,
And I wanted them to know
what I thought
because I thought.

So now I am old, and I've waited,
a lifetime I've waited, for the hole in
the garden wall. A lifetime I've waited
for a page I can fill and then keep, or
a page I can fill and erase,
and new pages appear
on a screen.
A lifetime I've waited to reach with
my hand and touch fingers that reach
across waters and cultures
and time zones,
a time to find souls just like me,
souls with a promise to keep,
souls wide awake
when the world is asleep.

Captcha the Intruders

Maybe you love to play a certain game online, but you can't get into the game room until you prove that you're a human. Yes, that is the criteria. It's like peeking through a little oval window in a twenties saloon and telling a goon, "God sent me. Here's my DNA."

Wikipedia says Captcha is a contrived acronym for Completely Automated Public Turing Test to tell Computers and Humans Apart. Really. I'm not kidding. But to me, Captcha sounds a lot like Gotcha.

So, when you sign in to your game room, with your password of course, letters and numbers pop up, and you must type them into another box. Apparently typing is the one thing that a computer can't do, so here's where we sort the men from the boys, or the real people from the wannabes. And your high school record of a hundred words a minute (errors discounted) does not impress. There can be no errors. If you type it wrong, the door slams shut, and you feel like a contestant on the *Gong Show*.

If you can't do anything else in your whole life, you can at least be human. If you fail that test, well it's hard to describe how that feels.

But let me tell you why it's a hard test to pass. The letters and numbers that pop up are all different sizes, and they look like they've been smashed by an anvil so that a two looks like an S (or is it a Z?) and C followed by an I makes a D, or an I followed by a three looks like a B, or is it thirteen? Who knows? Three or four tries, maybe seven, and the door finally opens. You're in. It makes you feel shady, but at least you know you're still human.

Now about the other jokers who line up to share your monitor's screen, there are many. I think we've finally gotten rid of the little paperclip guy. You know, Mr. Clippit, who used to pop up in the corner of your screen and say, "It looks like you are writing a letter," and you said, "Well, duh."

He had no idea what you were doing. He was like a two-year-old who wants to help you make pancakes.

So we put him away, but I used to think Clippit might be an omen of Big Brother or otherworldly things to come. I could see him morphing into a Hal, popping up to say, “It looks like you are writing a dirty joke. May I clean it up for you?” or “It looks like you are writing a recipe. Can I stay for dinner?” or “It looks like you are wiring money from your bank account. I will complete that transaction for you.”

Uh huh. We are not so dumb, you know. We are humans, and we can prove it.

And now we have companies or individuals popping up on our screens wanting to manage our debt, consolidate it, eliminate it. Or, if you like being in debt, they will loan you more money to squander. There are those who offer cheap drugs, fail-proof diets, a harmonious mate, and a prolonged and perfect sex life. LOL. I repeat, LOL.

Computers are wonderful. They bring the world to you. And they teach you how to keep the world out. Just download a few expensive tech goons to watch your door, and no one gets in unless they can prove they are humans listed in your book of life.

Highlights of My Brilliant Smoking Career

I quit smoking in 1986. I'm not going to tell you how long I had smoked, but let's just say that I was tempted and carefully led into smoking by the culture of the forties and fifties. Everyone who was anyone smoked. Glamorous magazine ads featured smoking movie stars, society dames, and famous athletes. Other ads featured doctors in white coats who told us which cigarettes were "best" for us. Young women practiced their first draw in front of mirrors to look cool and experienced like the people in the pictures. Young men came home from World War II with a new habit because smokes were a standard ration to all overseas units.

None of us had the slightest idea we were making a long-term commitment. Nor did we know the long-term consequences. No one did, and we were slow to catch on when people began graduating to oxygen tanks … and, eventually, to satin-lined boxes.

Anyway, by now I was a grandmother. I had smoked through all of my child-raising years, and, as most smokers did, I simply overlooked the fact that our house was filled with smoke, our car was filled with smoke, and all our clothes, curtains, and carpets smelled like smoke. When my sons came home from a hard swim workout, I somehow didn't hear them say, "Mom, it hurts my lungs to walk back into this house." As I lit another after-dinner cigarette, I didn't notice my husband, a nonsmoker, sigh and leave to go for a walk. I was able to overlook the discomfort of others because I needed that next cigarette. I didn't want it. I needed it.

As with all smokers, I went from an occasional cigarette to a one-pack-a-day habit and then gradually close to a two-pack-a-day habit. It's the usual progression as one's dependence grows. By the eighties, I was becoming uncomfortable. I began to resent the way the habit made me look and feel, the taste in my mouth, the way others frowned at me, and my complete inability to stop the compulsion.

So how many times did I try, and how did I finally quit? Let me count the ways. No, I'll spare you by saying that I tried them all, and none of them worked for me until I signed up for a seminar at my local hospital. It was sponsored by Smokenders, Inc. and led by an interesting man who had just retired from the US Air Force and who had himself been freed from the habit by this program. Our group of fifteen to twenty people went through six weekly meetings in which we gained new understanding of our habit, set goals, and altered our routines while weaning ourselves gradually from nicotine (as we continued for four weeks to smoke cigarettes but with less and less nicotine content).

On quit day, four weeks into the course, with understanding at last and a new set of habits, I did in fact quit. Two more weeks of class helped me deal with stumbling blocks, and then I was a graduate ready to begin my challenging transition back into the real world.

When I had been free of nicotine for a year, my Smokenders instructor contacted me and gave me an opportunity to receive training and to become an instructor myself. In time I traveled to present seminars during those years when large corporations were making their buildings smoke-free and giving their employees an opportunity to quit smoking with professional help. I received assignments, sometimes spur of the moment, and found myself to be one of those faceless people who walk from plane to plane with a briefcase.

My business was teaching large classes of people how to quit smoking. I could not believe I was doing this. I was a Midwestern housewife, and I was no spring chicken, you know. My classes had fun guessing my age, and I don't think anyone ever got it right. But I had something to share, and age had nothing to do with it.

The one thing that saved me from my bad habit, the one thing over and above everything else, was a simple fact that I had learned from Jacqueline Rogers, pioneer in the field of cessation and founder of the Smokenders program. It explained everything to me.

A smoker thinks that he lights his next cigarette because he wants to. He doesn't. He lights his next cigarette because his nicotine level has gradually fallen, and now he needs to bring it back up to his "comfort level" with more nicotine. It is the nicotine already in his system that screams for more, that makes him watch the clock, pace the floor, and snip at others. It is the need for nicotine replacement that sends him out late at night in the middle of a storm for more and that makes him pack a carton for a weekend trip, just in case.

Once I understood this, I could lick the habit by lowering my nicotine, needing less and less, and eventually needing none, while forming new behavior patterns to avoid the traps.

One week our class gave up smoking after a meal. We were surprised how quickly we formed new habits of clearing the table and cleaning the kitchen quickly or going for a walk. One week we quit smoking in the car and then cleaned the interior of that car until it was immaculate. Some filled the ashtrays with potpourri. We narrowed our choices of where we could smoke, and of course we gradually quit smoking while on the phone or in a restaurant, at a picnic or a football game.

My last cigarette was smoked outside the back door. Maybe I chose that instinctively because it was the door I always went through to take out the garbage.

During my transition period, I helped myself a lot by starting new hobbies, tackling things I had never thought of doing before, things that required every bit of my attention. On the day I quit smoking, I sat down with needle and thread, a piece of linen, and an instruction book, and I began a piece of Danish embroidery called Hardanger. It was so complicated that I could not look away but was forced to look at the instructions, then down at my sewing, and I did this all day long until I realized that the sun had gone down, and I must turn on my lamp. In the next few months, I made a stack of collector's-item pieces, and they are a treasure to me today.

In Chicago I suggested sewing to a young girl who was struggling with her transition away from cigarettes, and she took it so seriously she discovered she had a talent for design. She showed up at her graduation, at the end of the course, in a gorgeous dress and hat she had designed and made herself.

A shy young man in another class in Chicago was missing meetings. I reached him by phone as I waited for my plane home and encouraged him to come back to class.

"I'm just not getting it," he said. "I don't think I belong."

We talked for a long time, and somewhere in the conversation I suggested he get more exercise. Whatever else helped to get this across I don't know, but he showed up the next week, his assignments completed, and told us he had joined a health club and was working out every day. By graduation time, he had not only quit smoking, he had toned his body and changed his appearance and his personality. No one knew him. But then most people in the class had changed their appearance. In a few weeks, the gray, haggard look was replaced by a normal skin tone and a brighter countenance. It was fun to watch.

All "my" smokers planned something special to do on quitting day to celebrate their freedom. One girl went up in a balloon, as she said, "to see a bigger picture for her life." One man took his wife on a picnic, complete with blanket, checkered cloth, French loaves, wine, and cheese … and this was memorable because it was a bleak winter day. In another class, two participants not only fell in love with their new smoke-free life but they fell in love with each other. On the day they quit smoking, they were married.

An executive showed up in a large class in Minneapolis. He had signed up to set an example for his employees but had no intention of quitting himself. To his surprise, he realized partway through the class that he had already done the hard work of freeing his body of nicotine, so he quit gladly, and that is when he truly became a way-shower.

It's been years since I travelled and helped smokers. But I've had good healthy years because of the decision I made to quit and the reinforcement I gave myself by teaching others. I have twenty-two family members, counting children, grandchildren (with spouses), and now great-grandchildren too. I'm glad to say that none of them smoke, and their houses may smell like shampoo or pizza or popcorn but never like smoke.

Most smokers can say they have tried to quit. Some become very good at trying to quit. Among those who actually do quit, most have a very strong motive. Mine was money. I am very careful with my money, and when I put about three hundred dollars on the line to attend that seminar, I put my whole heart into succeeding so I'd get my money's worth.

Now here is an interesting fact for all the smokers who believe they can still afford to buy cigarettes but can't afford to spend a tiny portion of that money to find a way to help themselves quit: In the years since I quit smoking, I have enjoyed good health. And to my amazement, using conservative figures, I have saved well over $70,000 that would have been spent on cigarettes! Invested, with compounded interest, well I can't even begin to do the math. As it is, I am not only richer financially but considerably richer in good health, good relationships, self-respect, and, certainly, in peace of mind.

* * * * * *

Smokenders seminars are still given in some large cities, and their reasonably priced do-it-yourself Quit Kit is available on their website, http://www.smokenders.com.

A Grandmother Speaks On Being a Talent Scout

This grandmother was reclining, watching TV, and on the verge of an afternoon nap when a zoo keeper on the *Animal Planet* TV show, holding a penguin and surrounded by penguins, said something that brought me straight up in my chair. He showed a bright-colored, rather crude drawing of a penguin and said, "This is what I drew when I was six and the teacher asked us to draw a picture of what we would like to do when we grew up."

"At six! Yes!" I murmured, and was up and at my computer in minutes, looking in My Documents for something I had written one rainy day and then tucked away, thinking perhaps it was a foolish notion. For what it's worth, now somewhat validated, here it is:

* * * * * *

I have an idea that our children tell us very early in their life what they would like to do when they grow up. Not in words, of course, but in their choices, in the things that give them joy consistently. Sometimes parents observe all this and steer their children in directions that will mean the most to them. Sometimes they miss it entirely, but the child succeeds anyway, going naturally in his own direction … or sometimes missing and then struggling for years to find the way back to his passion.

My experience told me a lot about this. I grew up on a farm in the Midwest during the Depression years. Money was scarce, and we learned to appreciate the smallest favors. I had a doll but very few toys. I created my toys. A cardboard box, poked with rows of holes and a string with a pencil on the end that fitted into the holes, became a switchboard. I was a telephone operator for hours on end, wearing earmuffs for my headpiece, pulling plugs in and out of my switchboard while voicing, "Number, please. How may I help you? Let me connect you." (I know you don't know what a telephone operator is, but use your imagination. We used to need them to connect our calls.)

When I was six, I was given my own room, and there I created a desk from an old side table. I loved to sit at my desk organizing my ideas, writing letters, stories, and poems. But there was never enough paper. I asked my mother for paper, and she gave me one sheet, because paper was precious to her too, and paper cost money.

In those days, we did not receive piles of toys, as children do now, and I know that I was thrilled and grateful for what I did receive. But looking back, I wonder why no one ever gave me paper. No one ever bought me a book.

I'm sure I missed a lot of clues that my children gave me too. Still, our eldest son, who used to raid closets and even the rag box, creating outlandish costumes, staging shows, and playing crude instruments he had bought at the dime store, ended up often on the stage as a musician and has a rehearsal/recording studio where he offers services to other musicians and also teaches guitar lessons. He was six when he began asking for his first guitar. He was seven when he belted out Gary Indiana as Winthrop in the high school production of *Music Man*.

Our youngest son drew a clear path. From two to four, he spent hours in a sand pile his father had created from a tractor tire filled with sand. He acquired a huge supply of plastic military figures, which he put into play with tanks and planes, fighting battles by the hour under the shady elm tree outside my kitchen window.

When he was six, I allowed him to walk several blocks downtown by himself. I held my breath, but he returned safely carrying a large box full of army and navy posters. He had visited both recruiting offices.

This boy set goals early and met requirements to be admitted to the United States Air Force Academy after graduation from high school. He became an officer in the Air Force, flying planes as he had always dreamed of doing. He served twenty-seven years, was nine times in Afghanistan and Iraq, and after retiring as a full colonel, now pilots commercial planes.

Our daughter became a nurse. She received her training a bit later in life, after marriage and children, and she found her way there by herself. I had no idea that she had given us early clues until one day I came across an old picture tucked away in a dresser drawer. It was a picture of her at … can you believe it? … the age of six.

She had created an emergency room in our basement. The picture shows her attending a patient (one of the neighbor kids, with others waiting in line) on a table created from an old door on two wooden sawhorses. She was listening to the heart of the patient with a stethoscope from her toy nurse set, and the patient's leg was elevated and wrapped in towels. Need I say that she became a paramedic, then a registered nurse, and that she specialized in emergency care?

Well, you see, we could talk about how simple it all looks in hindsight. But I mention my little theory to young mothers along with a caution to use measured foresight. Children have some serious playing to do and must not be troubled with thoughts about their future careers, unless of course a child is a genius, in which case there will have been ample clues and unusual steps to consider.

For the average child, the kind most of us have, play is everything. Children are not in their thoughts but in their feelings. They are not into thinking but into doing, and they learn by doing. If their fun gives you insight, perhaps your sensitivity will lead you to make the path easier for the ones you love. This may mean signing them up for lessons of some sort, or it may mean not signing them up for lessons! I'd say if they roll their eyes and sigh a lot at the piano, it's not their forte.

Watch for what they love! What do they do when they are alone? What do you absolutely have to drag them away from to come to the table or to go to bed? What do they want to do on weekends or on long, hot days of summer? (Video games are addictive and don't count for this purpose.)

You may spot that special desire, that inborn talent, but remember this: what you observe will remain a secret in your heart of hearts. I should think that no one squelches a child's desire more than pushy parents. Let it be the secret that they will uncover as they go along.

For instance, if a child loves history, take him on a summer vacation to historic spots for the whole family to enjoy but not to prime his pump. It will accomplish the same thing.

Along the way, as they grow, children will be influenced by their peers, by television and movies, by adult pressures, and many other things, so that the clearest messages they send will be those from their hearts before the age of seven.

So watch and listen, but I'd advise not to take an isolated incident as an omen of the future. I made the girls' basketball team, not because I was an athlete but because the coach was short one girl. I won the county spelling bee, but I was never meant to write a dictionary.

You see what I mean.

Their Words Walk with Me

Decisions have always challenged me. As a child, I would stand for ages at an ice-cream counter weighing chocolate against vanilla. No wonder when I began to make life decisions it was painful for me, and sometimes also for those who cared about me.

Just out of college, I delayed signing a teaching contract until the last moment because I couldn't decide between offers. "Make your choice," my mother urged. "Wherever you go, it will be new to you, but you will get used to it. You will just get used to it."

Later I dallied in naming my babies. "What if he doesn't like the name?" I asked. "Or what if the other kids make a funny nickname of it?"

"Just choose a name, any name that you like," my mother would say. "You will get used to it. You will just get used to it, and so will everyone, and no one would ever think of changing it because the child will become that person." She was right of course, and years later one of my sons came to me and thanked me for choosing the name he would have chosen for himself.

"You'll get used to it." Such a simple piece of advice, and I never heard my mother give it to anyone but me, because I was the one who needed just that. She used it to prod me into quicker decisions, and forced me to see that once I put my foot on a path, I was on my way to somewhere and that most of the time if I didn't like it I could change my direction then.

My brother had other helpful words for me. While hesitant about my own moves, I could often see clearly what others should do, and friends valued my opinions. But I was afraid my advice might lead someone in the wrong direction. I just too often felt responsible for others.

"You are not responsible for their actions," my brother would say. "No matter what you say, when it comes down to it, people do what they want to do."

"No they don't," I argued. "My friend does things because her husband wants her to do them."

"Then she is doing what she wants to do," he said. "She wants to do what her husband wants her to do." He was right, of course. People do what they want to do.

My father taught me patience as only a patient person can, by being patient. "Give it time," he would say. He was a quiet, thoughtful man and moved slowly on things, quite unlike my mother who moved into full-blown action on impulse and whose desire for change forced her to rearrange the furniture constantly.

It took me years to see that my natural disposition was more like my father's and that trying to emulate my mother put enormous pressure on me. But at the same time, I needed some of her gumption in my survival kit.

I think of my family as a very special group of souls I was privileged to learn and grow with. Can you imagine walking through life without strong people near to advise you and to regroup with at the end of a day … a year … a lifetime? I had many teachers but none so direct and truthful as those who sat with me around our kitchen table.

A sibling will tell you when you have a slip showing or need a breath mint in life, and parents will smile when you do well and frown when you don't. But you will learn as well by watching what works and what doesn't work for them in their lives, and somehow it's easier to see through a situation you are not yourself involved in. You will learn by osmosis the very strengths that each family member brought to the unit, and you will also learn early to spot their weaknesses and the consequences they cause.

So they teach by example without ever knowing it, but each family member teaches too by delivering to you, just when you need it, or perhaps over and over, the angel message they were meant to bring just for you.

Early memories are the strong ones later in life, so is it any wonder that now in retirement my parents, long gone, sometimes walk beside me with their words?

When my husband died, I began to wonder if I should give up the big, rambling house where we raised our children and move to a town house or a condo apartment, but the thought stopped me cold. "Give it time," said my dad in that peculiar space where my loved ones sometimes return to comment or to counsel. "You don't have to decide today. You'll know when it's time."

"In the end, you'll do what you want to do," said my brother, also long gone.

"You'll be fine. Whatever you decide you'll get used to it. You'll just get used to it," said my mother from her place in my heart.

And so they helped me to get through another transition, and as you know, I did sell the house and buy a lovely smaller place. From this, I know that if the time eventually comes when I must consider entering a retirement home or a care center, my mother's voice will comfort me with "You'll be fine. You'll get used to it … you'll just get used to it," and, of course, I know that I will.

Thanksgiving 1947 with my birth family
Gene and I are there (lower right) to announce our engagement.

About Time

The clock doesn't slow down when we do. Those crazy numbers just click away in the same, old circle at the same, old pace.

We say time goes faster when we are having fun, yet we say time goes faster as we grow older. Is that fun? Go figure.

Time seems to go faster when we're busy. Time goes slower when we are bored. So explain why time goes faster now that I'm not so busy.

Many people have put forth scientific theories regarding how our brains record our experience and give us our concept of time. One simple explanation is that a day in the life of a small child is long in proportion to the time he has spent on earth. So that explains why a day in my life now is so short.

I have been a child, and I have been a senior, and I'd say while I used to run and play every day for about ninety-six hours, I now get up, sneeze, and go back to bed. Thanksgiving falls a few days after the Fourth of July.

Not to be discouraged. It's like money. When we have a lot of it and a source of income, we may be tempted to spend without thought, without plan, because there will always be more. When money is scarce, we begin to realize our part in the scheme of things.

Nothing is more precious than time. It is all we have. Perhaps realizing that is one of the major lessons in life. And there's no such thing as a lesson failed. It is always a lesson learned. As we say, everything comes in time.

LAUGHING

Funny's Good but Not to Die For

I'd like to write simple, understated humor from my own experience, because life's a hoot to the one living it, and funny things happen along the way. Unfortunately not all are still funny the next day, and few are even remembered. Repeating funny things I did could well have people laughing at me. I'd rather they laugh with me, and the trick to that, of course, is self-effacing humor. People like self-effacing humor because it makes them feel better about themselves. Putting myself down royally could work for me. While people laugh at me because I'm so stupid, they could also be laughing with me because I'm so smart I know I'm stupid.

I'd like to be Garrison Keillor, but that spot's taken out here in the Midwest, where that Minnesota guy does live broadcasts on National Public Radio. And anyway I'm a woman, I'm not that funny, and I'm too good looking. Now there I go again. You can't be self-effacing while being self-aggrandizing. One cancels the other. Anyway, I finally figured out you can't be self-effacing until you're somebody. People like to laugh at somebodies who wink while pretending they're nobodies. But if you're already a nobody, it's pretty hard to talk yourself down to a lower level.

For another thing, it's been well established that stories about Lutherans and Catholics in Minnesota are funny. Try talking about Lutherans and Catholics in New York or California and see how many laughs you get!

I'd like to be Erma Bombeck, God rest her soul. Hilarious things happened in my home too as the kids were growing up, but somehow they were not so funny in the retelling. As someone has said about comedians, some say funny things, and some say things funny. Erma was born to do both. I wish she had been my neighbor. Wouldn't that be a blast?

Or would it? Johnny Carson was funny in front of millions, not funny away from the camera and out in the multitudes, but funny again with a small, select group of friends. So his humor was meant for a mike and camera or a rare face-to-face, yet I saw little of it in public or in print. But here's something funny. I live in his old hometown and met him once when he was here for a visit. Well, he didn't exactly track me down or anything. It was me who stopped him on the street with my hand extended, and of course he shook it and murmured a greeting. It wasn't anything funny, but then he didn't know he was going to run into me.

I'd like to say funny things about politics, but the political field isn't funny anymore. It's nasty, desperate, and downright frightening. If I really wanted to make people laugh, I would try saying something serious about politics.

There was that one time when I wrote something serious … and brought down the house. It was in a freshman journalism class taught by a local city editor, a hardened, old cynic. Our first assignment was to write a simple account of a wedding for the society page. A week later, the editor came into class, slammed our papers down, glared at us, gave a big sigh, and singled out my paper.

"This is the one," he said. "This is the wedding of the year." He stood reading it to himself and then said, "Now, here's the good part: 'and after "Oh Perfect Love" was sung by a friend of the bride, rings were exchanged, and the marriage was consummated at the altar.'"

Okay, so I made an unfortunate error in my youthful innocence, but it taught me something too. I'll bet when you read that last sentence you were viewing a mental picture of the wedding, and that's what made the corners of your mouth go up.

Words create laughs when they sound funny to our inner or our outer ear, or when they draw a funny picture on our mental screen. They also grab us by the funny bone when they carry a double meaning that delivers a surprise. The humor of children is full of puns, full of surprises, and we never outgrow that need to giggle, nor our adult need to chuckle, snort, guffaw, and occasionally roll on the floor, pounding our chest and begging for mercy.

But the kind of humor I'd be content to write just brings a grin, a knowing smile. Smiles feel good, cost little, and stay on the face longer. Smiles heal. If I ever figured out how to write really funny, I would put it out with instructions: take one paragraph upon arising, one after each meal, one at bedtime … and see your doctor at once if a laugh lasts longer than four hours.

The Granny Nest

Now that I'm older,
I have my own chair
That nobody uses
But me. They don't dare.
And next to my chair
Is a very good light,
A window for daytime,
A floor lamp for night.

And next to my light
Is a very fine table
That's loaded with thimbles,
A guide for the cable,
An emery board
And a nail undercoat,
My tissues, my fan,
My own TV remote,
A puzzle or two
(With the answers in back),
A book of short stories,
Some fruit for a snack.

I'm no longer looking
For men or old geezers,
But always I'm looking
For glasses or tweezers,
My lotions, my letters,
The things I like best.
So I've gathered them up,
And I've built me a nest.

It's here I create
With my needles and pins
And, when no one is looking,
Pluck hairs from my chins.

Doris Markland

Poems for Fun

Pocket Pleas

These days when I'm shopping
I notice, and sadly,
The loss of a feature
We're needing so badly.
We've outgrown the eras
Of hankies and lockets
But never our penchant
For generous pockets.
We like them in blouses,
We like them in shirts,
We like them in slacks,
And we like them in skirts.
We need them for tissues,
We need them for dimes,
We need them for hands
In the most awkward times.
We need them for keys
So they'll never get lost.
We need them for records
Of what something cost.
As we need the science
It takes to make rockets,
We need the return
Of the folks who make pockets.
So these lines are written
To beg the designers
Please honor the wishes
Of pocketless whiners.
We know you need profits,
We know you watch cost,
But consider: without us,
Your business is lost.

Keeping Abreast

I remember breasts
When they were not the "in" thing
Yet were furthest out.
I had great aunts who, when they sat,
Had only knees for laps.
I glimpsed the hidden flesh sometimes
When ladies loosened corsets,
Pulled the shades,
To breathe in comfort for their naps.

I remember bosoms,
Mounds in rows across the pew
On Sunday morning,
Heaving heavy, rugged crosses,
Sleeping infants in their sin.
There were no pillows ever made
That better cradled rosy cheeks
Or rocked to heaven souls all locked
And diapered in.

I remember busts
When they were busting,
Hung from shoulder straight to waistline,
Hung with lorgnettes, lace, and lockets,
Proud and innocent at that,
In a time when breast meant mother,
And no husband and no brother
Thought too much of it
Was anything but fat.

I remember figures
Full and blooming in their aprons,
Stirring applesauce and gravy,
Frying chicken on the range,

And no one made comparisons
With sisters tall and willowy
Or cousins slight and trim
Or thought it strange.
What women were they simply were
And couldn't change.

Breasts are not invented
By an agency in Hollywood
Or molded by a maiden's training bra;
They just grow as they were seeded
To be there when they are needed,
And Dad and all the kids
Think they're just fine.

Ad Lib

My TV set is miserable.
It whines, and it complains
Of headaches, backaches, blisters,
Upset stomach, menstrual pains.
It burns and itches, smarts and stings,
And has a funny smell
In places I don't care
To have it mention, show, or tell.

My TV set's in agony
And needs a new idea
On how to heal its hemorrhoids
And stop its diarrhea.
It's tired and needs a respite
From exploring all the fads
Of panties, belts, and tampons,
Maxi-bras, and mini-pads.

My TV set's in danger!
I have had it up to here!
If it's sick, I'm getting rid of it
And reading books this year.
If it's negative and nasty,
I will show it out the door.
The world is full of downers;
That is not what TV's for.

It may serve me up the latest news
In far exotic places,
Boston Symphony or interviews
With positive new faces.
It may stir me with fine drama,
Laugh with Carson, Hope, and Lewis,
But it should do something for us
And should not do something to us.

It may show us homemade cookies,
Razor blades and cars and watches,
But it may not show us underwear
And make us look at crotches.
It may picture mighty earthquakes,
Mountain rivers freely rushing,
But not the ones in kitchen drains
Or in a toilet flushing!

I know TV must sell to make
The bread to feed the set,
But it's selling me on selling.
I may sell my TV yet!

Note: I recently found this tucked in a book, and I remembered writing it many years ago. In the early days of TV, we were shocked that the advertising brought right into our living rooms things we never talked about. We found the ads shocking!

Much the same can be said for the verse about breasts. In earlier days, they really weren't a topic of conversation or a requirement for entertainment.

Saturday Evening Postings

Maybe we all need someone to idolize at times. The one I idolized for years was Richard Armour. He was a writer of light verse, the one who wrote things like "Shake and shake the ketchup bottle. Some will come and then a lott'l." And this one, which is so apt today: "Politics, it seems to me, For years or all too long, Has been concerned with right or left, Instead of right or wrong."

The only periodicals I saw in our home as a child were farming magazines. I had other interests, and when we went to visit my grandparents, I made a beeline for the oak library table in the front hall and grabbed the *Saturday Evening Post* before my brother did. I'd plop down on the living room carpet, open the magazine, and flip to the page called "Post Scripts." And then I'd look for Richard Armour, and I'd almost always find him there.

He was well educated, a college professor, a writer of books, but I think he was best known, like Ogden Nash, for writing funny verses. Another of his best remembered was this: "Nothing attracts the mustard from wieners As much as the slacks just back from the cleaners."

Although I did some writing through my adult years, in particular writing verse for Hallmark cards and other greeting companies, I was well into my later years before I dared to try to do what Richard Armour did. A lot of my attempts ended up in the wastebasket, but a few found their way, by some miracle of luck, to the very page where I once found my idol … Post Scripts, in the *Saturday Evening Post*. It was almost like coming home.

My poems in Post Scripts:

Wait!

In waiting rooms
I'm often vexed
When I am not
The one who's "next!"
Unless I'm there
To get a shot,
And then I'm very
Glad I'm not.

The Workout

"Exercise to stay in shape"
Is advice that I'm
Really in doubt of.
The reason I'm here
Should be perfectly clear:
I've a shape that I want
To work out of.

Counterpoint

Approaching the counter
I unload my items
And I do the talking today.
Flashing my Visa
And palming a twenty,
"Paper or plastic?" I say."

Marilee We'd Roll Along

You know what more families need? What more nations need, and maybe what the United Nations needs? People like my friend Marilee.

Widowed young, Marilee raised four children by herself, and very well. I often wondered how she did it without a father to discipline.

"For instance," I once asked her, "what did you do when the kids came screaming to you, bloodied and bawling, each blaming another for starting the fracas?"

"Oh, that was easy," she said. "I sat them down around the dining room table with tablets and pencils, and I said, 'This is very serious. We must get to the bottom of it.'"

Then, looking around the table at each one, Marilee said, in her very serious voice, "You are to write what happened, from the very beginning, telling who said what and who did what. Leave out not a single detail, as I will need all the facts before I decide who must be punished."

After admonishing "no talking," she left the room and went about her day.

"It worked," she told me. The wonderful peace of silence fell upon the house, and when she peeked into the dining room, ten minutes later, it was always empty.

A Smutty Story

"Gourmets pay big $$ to eat fungus farmers throw away," read the headline, along with a corny second line, "There's a fungus among us!" Well, forget the fungus. It was the $$ that caught my eye, and I went on to read about an Illinois farmer who used to pay to rid his corn crop of the fungus called "smut" but now was making a bundle as a "smut peddler," selling the stuff at $2 to $3 a pound. Chefs use it, and it's a key ingredient in many Mexican dishes, I read.

Now I grew up with a mother who wove rugs in her cozy little loom house, who had chickens for egg money, and was a stringer for a number of newspapers, so it was my heritage to stay at home after I married but to find every possible way to make an honest buck for my mad money. And, remember, this was long before eBay.

So I thought about that smut, which, frankly, I had been curious about since encountering it myself when I carried lunches to the field workers as a child. So I approached my husband, the gentleman farmer, and asked if he could please locate and bring home some smut to me. He looked a bit shocked but replied, "Certainly, if I can find it. And how do you want it?"

"In a plain brown wrapper," I replied, for obvious reasons.

When he came home, to my surprise, he bore two ears of corn, each with an appendage of gray stalactites (or is it stalagmites?), that is, something growing in a way that arouses suspicion and suggests that someone somewhere can charge admission for people just to see these things. To eat them must cost double.

Where they erupted off the surface of the corn kernels, they were light gray, smooth, shiny, and probably somewhat comparable to mushrooms that pop up from the spongy earth beneath an old oak tree. Only, once erupted, the gray parasites tend to grow scruffy with age, eventually turning black, and later disintegrating into a fine powder. So I knew right away that, just like people, you want to enjoy this stuff when it's young and good looking.

The gentleman farmer was leaving on a fishing trip, and this seemed a good time, home alone, to try out the delicacy. If I died, it would be a highly dramatic finish. ("Local housewife smitten by smut.")

So I approached the ears delicately with a knife, cutting away the black parts and retrieving the fresh, young portions. I smelled them. They smelled like corn.

As to their edibility, I needed a second opinion, so I went to the computer. *Who is an expert on smut? Ah, the County Extension Office*, and here I read their answer to a poster's question:

> Most likely your corn is infected with the pathogen Ustilago maydis, more widely known as common smut. Common smut is a fungus that typically is found on the ears and tassels of the corn plant in conspicuous dark galls that replace kernels and may reach several inches in diameter (although most samples brought to the Extension office are about one inch or so in diameter). You will see them in clusters on your ear of corn. While they ruin your ears of corn they are not harmful to humans. Corn smut is considered a delicacy in Mexico. One has to eat it before the spores become ripe, when the insides are still moist and the gall is white to gray on the outside.

So far so good. Now I'm sitting in my kitchen staring at a dish full of funny stuff and wondering what to do next. I called a friend, and she said, "You want to know how to cook *what*?"

I called my mother, who was ninety-three, alive and well in Iowa, and she said, "Our kind of people do not eat smut."

Now I remembered that I'd heard smut compared in some ways to truffles, those expensive fungi that are rooted out of the soil in France by pigs, so I asked myself, "What would a chef do?" Well, but of course. He would sauté.

So I set the table with a stunning placemat and napkin, silver, and my best china and crystal. Now for the wine. Red or white with smut? I settled for white zinfandel, which is really pink.

I had prepared a small salad and cut some homemade bread, and now approached the stove for the final preparation. Ah. A lump of butter, then the delicate morsels, which sizzled and bounced about, turning slightly brown and looking every bit like food. A little seasoning and onto a plate, nicely arranged with a garnish of red pepper strips, and to the table. I began to eat immediately, before apprehension could set in. A bite of smut, a bite of bread. Now and then a sip of wine. I would eat the salad later (very European).

I ate it all, knowing that if one must acquire a taste, it cannot be done in one bite. Neither the taste nor the texture was unpleasant, and the flavor was perhaps familiar. In fact, if I had to say, I could say that smut tasted a good deal like … well, like day-old corn.

Which reminds me, oddly, of my childhood fear that I might bite into an apple and find a worm. My brother used to say that wouldn't be bad. Worse would be biting into an apple and finding half a worm. No problem, my mother assured us. The worm had eaten nothing but apple and would taste exactly like apple. And so it did, I am sure, as I must have eaten plenty of worms in my day without even knowing.

But never before had I eaten smut. Nor since.

Lightening Moments

Housewife's Confession

I've stolen moments for a nap,
Snatched bargains at the mall.
I've raided kitchens in the night,
Robbed Peter to pay Paul.
I've high-jacked cars to fix a tire,
I've rolled and pinched the dough,
And, when I'm shopping,
Swiped more cards
Than you will ever know.

The Tired Help

I hired a girl
To clean the house,
And now I'm almost lame.
I stayed up half the night
To get it clean
Before she came.

Culinary Itch

I often get the itch to cook,
but I can never match
my Grandma
'cause she skips the itch
and starts right out
from scratch.

The Editor

I mentioned
I'm not writing
For posterity,
I'm writing
For prosperity,
And he said,
"Well I see
From what you've
Sent to us,
You can't be
Very prosperous."

Up Close and Personal

Oh what a nice, big dog you have,
What grace, what powerful jaws!
I love him … till he jumps on me,
And then he gives me paws.

Dermatheology

When I said "Oh, Lord,
Make me skinny,"
I thought that the change
Would be good.
But I didn't grow thin,
I just grew extra skin.
I think I was misunderstood.

X-Spendable

I saved my money,
Cent by cent,
But it was dollars
That I spent.
I saved bucks for
A rainy day,
But then the flood
Washed them away.
I think I need
A better plan,
But savers save
As savers can.

It Figures

To learn the metric measure
All at once became a "must"
When I found that it would give me
Eighty-seven in the bust;
But the laws of human symmetry
Were not to be denied,
For my hips spread out to ninety-six
Full centimeters wide.

PTA

Teacher's report
that is sure to
please mothers:
does all his
homework
and plays well
with others.

Teacher's report
that sounds good
to a dad:
kid made the team
and is not doing bad.

The Difference between a Jackass

Until the other night, I hadn't known or cared much to know what a jackass is, technically. Then someone had to ask.Here's the story as told by one of the guys.

Ed Hartman, a friend of mine, has this thing going with his neighbor, kind of a contest to see who can pull off the best practical joke on the other. Halloween stuff, but they don't wait for Halloween.

When Ed found his barbecue tied to his television antenna last year, he got a bunch of guys together one night, and they hauled all his neighbor's patio furniture up onto his roof.

This year Ed found an old backhouse plunked at the edge of his pool. Now he's looking for a good comeback, and he brought it up after a gin game in Doc Adams's basement.

Doc said he knows a fellow out in the country has a new, little burro, and maybe Ed could borrow that and tie it to his neighbor's front door.

"What's he got a burro for?" someone asked.

"Beats me," said Doc. "It's a homely, little cuss."

"Say, Doc," piped up Hartman, "you're a vet. What's the difference anyway between a donkey, a burro, a jackass, and a mule?"

Doc grinned and opened his mouth, but Jim Fischer cut in. "Well," he said, "I know what a mule is. It's a cross between a jackass and a horse. Right, Doc?"

"Right. It's a cross between a jackass and a mare, and it's sterile. Male or female, either one, sterile."

"You mean once you're a mule, that's the end of the line, eh?" Fischer seemed concerned. "No one's pushing a mule for hanky-panky in the next coral then. No wonder mules are so darn contrary."

Everyone laughed, and Doc brought more coffee. "Anyone know what a hinny is?" he asked. No one did, so he went on "A hinny's out of a female ass bred by a stallion."

"Hinny?" asked Hartman. "Sure you don't mean a jenny?"

"Well actually," said Doc, "a jennet is a term sometimes used interchangeably with hinny. Bardot is another name, a French name. But when we say jenny, we mean a female ass, the counterpart of a jack."

Fischer hooted "Bardot? As in Bridgit? Man I could make a comment, but, as Johnny Carson says, I wouldn't touch that one with a fork."

"Wait a minute," I interrupted. Not that I cared, but still I like to get things once and get them straight. "A mule is produced by a jackass and a female horse. A male horse and a female ass produce a hinny. In other words, a jackass isn't a breed but just a way of saying a male ass."

A nod from Doc. He was enjoying the conversation and rather thankful they were drinking coffee and not beer.

I continued, clicking them off on my fingers, "And horses have horses, donkeys have donkeys, burros have burros, asses have asses, and mules have nothing."

"As a rule," Doc said. "Oh they have been known to reproduce, but it's rare. Mules are workers. They can work all day and never get tired and never get sick. Mules are so valuable that's why people keep jackasses, just so they can get mules."

"Then what's a donkey?" Hartman asked, cutting off Fischer, who was probably going to say that jackasses have all the fun.

"Well, if you must know," said Doc, "I guess I'd have to say a donkey's an ass of another kind. Domesticated, of course. There are all kinds of asses, you know."

"Ain't it the truth?" This from Fischer.

"And a burro?" I asked.

"Same thing," Doc said. "It's just a little donkey with a Spanish name. They got a lot of those down in the Southwest and in Mexico."

We were at the door when Hartman turned and said, "Doc, do you really know what you're talking about? I'll bet you haven't been called out into the country to treat a jackass for years."

"Don't know that I ever have," said Doc, "but I see a lot of 'em around town. They're a scroungy lot. Ask a lot of questions and play bum gin."

Note: I know. It's an unusual topic for me, and this is the only fiction in this book. But I heard a conversation something like this once, and it led me to research the topic and write it up as a story. Just a little fun for me, after I put the kids to bed back in the sixties.

Snippets

I always smile when I remember our family Thanksgiving in 1976.

Our three-year-old grandson came to me and asked if he could say the grace before dinner, and of course I said yes. It would be the prayer that many young children say: "Thank you, God, for the world so sweet. Thank you, God, for the food we eat. Thank you, God, for the birds that sing. Thank you, God, for everything."

When we'd gathered around the table, I nodded to Jason, and he delivered his prayer. He'd forgotten some of the words, but in doing so, he made it even more appropriate for Thanksgiving as he said:

"Thank you, God, for the world so sweet.
Thank you, God, for the bird we eat. Amen."

* * * * * *

Some years ago I was so eager to use my new digital camera that I snapped my first picture with a minimum of instruction, then hurried to my computer to download and view it.

There, on screen, was my daughter, sitting on a chair by the window just as I had seen her a few moments before. Then she stood up and walked off the screen. I almost fainted.

I hadn't known my camera had a setting for taking a one-minute movie, but I had found it.

When Grandma Said the F-F-Forbidden Word

I never said the F word until I was almost sixty, and then only as an experiment in linguistics. Not that I was unaware of the word, but it just wasn't part of my conscious vocabulary. I didn't say the word because I didn't think the word, so it wasn't there in my mind, ready and waiting to be puked out on any occasion. Perhaps I had also never said the word because of a dim primal fear that something terrible would happen if I did. Such was my teaching.

As a matter of fact, I had to work my way up to it by learning to say another dread word first as a sort of trial run. I remember being at a social function and noticing several people gathered at one end of the room with their drinks, and the whole group suddenly exploding in laughter. They laughed so hard that they had to set their drinks down so they could wipe their eyes or hold their sides. I was wondering what could be so funny when one of them came over to me and said, "Do you know what your husband just said? He said that you wouldn't say sh** if your mouth was full of it."

I was really embarrassed but, more than that, nonplussed to think that people found that funny. I thought and thought about this incident, asking myself how I had become so out of step with society.

So then, on another occasion when we were with friends for an evening, and the host asked me what I would like to drink, I took a deep breath and, in front of everyone, blurted, "Anything would be fine. I guess I don't really give a sh**."

If you think they laughed before, you should have heard them now. I figured it was a no-win situation, especially when we came home, and my husband lit into me. "How could you talk like that?" he asked. "You sounded like some kind of slut."

"Well, you can't have it both ways," I said, and just saying that helped me see down a long corridor that women have walked in this kind of confusion. We're damned if we do, and we're damned if we don't, and I damn well know I never said damn until I was at least forty-five.

So on to the F word. I finally said it in my kitchen, standing there alone, experimenting with the sound. I said the word over and over and found that it fell into a rhythm. The front teeth over the lower lip, and then the back of the tongue to the roof of the mouth. It made a rolling motion and a sound that was almost onomatopoetic. A gut-level word, no doubt about that, and soft when murmured but as an insult or a curse, absolutely vicious. The F sound can hiss like a cat and the K can bruise like the slam of a door, a deep assault to one's sensitivities.

Still, for all its strident misuse as a noun, an adjective, an expletive, and more, as a verb it has honesty. It is more correct to use this word to describe the mating function than it is to say "We made love." No one can make love, and to say so is a form of heresy. Love is. We can feel it, we can share it, but we cannot create it.

When I was young, the F word wasn't bandied about much. The word certainly wasn't an insult or something wished onto others or others' mothers. People did it, but they didn't talk about it. In fact, if they needed to refer to it, that's exactly how they said it. They said, "We did it." And when things went wrong, people muttered rats, darn, shucks, or … in fits of extreme anger … son of a bitch!

I still say shucks and darn, not because I am so puritan but because I'm comfortable in my rut. My kids have heard me say the sh** word once or twice when I dropped something on my toe, but after the first time, it lost its power, and no one noticed. They have never heard me say the F word, and I don't intend that they should.

So for me, the word still has power. If I, being my sweet, innocent self, were to walk into a room right now and come out with the F word, there would be a sudden deafening silence that I could use to my advantage. But that can only happen once. So I keep the word somewhere back in the vault for now, saving it for that one big, shattering emergency when I will need everyone's undivided attention.

Tech Talk

Sign of the Times

The next time you plan a vacation,
Perhaps you should learn how to spell.
The note on your window
"Gone Phishing"
Is not going over so well.

He-Mail (or E-Male)

It's clear you don't
Know me from Adam.
Your mail for a sir
Reached a madam.
The products you're selling
Are rather repelling,
And I couldn't use
If I had 'em.

Textception

To be modern in our culture
And communicate with peers,
Let your fingers do the talking
And your peepers be your ears.
Except when you are driving,
Then please choose a safer mode.
Keep your fingers on the wheel
And keep your peepers on the road.

The Juggler

An act that I see all too often,
Although it's a little bizarre,
Is the young miss who juggles
A Big Mac with french fries,
A Coke, her mascara,
An iPod, a hairbrush,
Her lipstick, and cell phone
While talking and driving a car.

Literati

I'm having words with people
In South Africa, Peru,
Barcelona, Buenos Aires,
Kandahar, and Kathmandu.
With thoughts of being worldly
I never thought I'd dabble,
But I'm finding others just like me,
Online and hooked on Scrabble.

Ah Love

If we had not been born so soon,
If we were young today,
Just think how different things would be
In what we'd do and say.
We might have met on the Internet.
We both might be tattoo-ed.
You'd call me baby-baby,
And I would call you dude.

We'd make our dates on cell phones.
We'd even smooch online.
"Our song" would be staccato rap,
And beer would be our wine.
You'd text me your proposal.
We'd coordinate our brains.
I'd use my thumbs to answer
While I am changing lanes.

Maybe we were innocent,
Or maybe we were dumb.
But touch was just a promise
Of things to later come,
And marriage was a contract
To honor and obey
While overlooking challenges
That just won't go away.

Ah love, it's always precious,
No matter, don't you know?
But, gee, I'm glad we had it all
A few decades ago.

LOVING

Come to Mother

Here we are, my little one,
Alone at last, we two,
And my eyes are full of wonder
At the pure delight of you
Stretching, yawning, stirring
On your tiny flannelette,
With arms and legs like petals
Of a rose not opened yet.
I count the toes and fingers,
Touch the tender, wrinkled skin,
Explore your new, sweet baby scent
And lovingly breathe in.
As best I can I tuck you back
Into your cozy fold.
I kiss and gently take you up
Into my arms to hold,
From every fiber of my being
Softly calling, "Come to Mother,"
As then we meet and, heart to heart,
We recognize each other.

Note: I wrote this poem to describe my first moments with my first child, a beautiful little girl. It became a favorite with Hallmark customers and was published on more than one card. It was also published in one of their books. I happened upon the book in a shop and bought a stack, so that I had a copy to give to the mothers when each of my grandchildren and my great-grandchildren were born.

Evening Star

Dear little baby, late surpriser,
Sent when I am older, wiser,
I know who you are.
Our fairy angels waved a wand,
And here you are from the beyond,
A newborn star.
What will you teach us?
Patience? Love?
Are you another chance above
The toil and tears
Of middle years,
A chance to make things right?
It won't be easy, that I know,
But, little star, you came to glow
For heaven knew we need you so
And sent your light.

Grandchildren

I want them near
When they are small,
When their eyes are full of wonder
And they think with their hearts,
When they are totally honest
And remember everything
That's said to them
Exactly
As
It
Was
Said.

I want them near
When they are trusting,
When they take my hand
And walk into adventure
Without question,
When my lap is their comfort,
My home is their castle,
And "I" am ageless
And wonderful.

Two-Part Harmony

When I was small,
I sat in church with Grandma.
Wintertime we snuggled close,
Summertime we fanned.
Where the sun fell
On our laps, she laid
Her linen handkerchief,
Knotted in one corner
To form a doll for me;
And from a packet in her
Purse, she gave a tiny
Square of licorice
For my tongue
To keep me quiet
Till we stood and sang.
And that was best,
Grandma and me
In two-part
Harmony.

Doris Markland

That's When I'll Be There

In the year of my eightieth birthday, I began to give thought to the urgings of my children that I clear the shelves and closets of our big house. I'm sure they thought it would ease the transition when their dad and I move to a smaller place, but I'm even more certain they thought it would make it easier for them when I am no longer here.

How much easier they will never know, I thought, as I hauled things to the garage for my spring rummage sale. I was selling the clothes, appliances, and doodads that didn't sell at my fall rummage sale or on my eBay offerings. It was sad to see how little value was attached by other people to things that had meant so much to me. It was painful to see them pick up something I valued and then put it down as if it were not worth considering. Even worse were the moments when someone held up a sterling silver gravy boat, a hand-embroidered tablecloth, and a crystal vase, asking, "Would you take fifty cents for all of this?" Indeed! But I swallowed my pride and waded through closet after closet, shelf after shelf, asking myself, "Can I live without this? Can I use this in a condo? Can I use it in (gulp) a nursing home?"

Still scrounging for more items the day before the sale, I found on a forgotten shelf a small church made of marbles. I took the dusty little church upstairs to clean. A few of the marbles were missing or broken, and I remembered the church had fallen off a shelf in the family room. Now I had to decide whether it was worth fixing. I knew I could probably locate a few of the old-fashioned red marbles at an antique store and could bake them to create a crackled effect as my mother had done when she made the church for me years ago … actually, as I think of it, about the time of her eightieth birthday.

The thought of my mother always makes me smile. Oh, what an energetic person she was. And creative. It was her nature, but it was also her need. Times were hard in her years as a young farmwife, and soon, in addition to helping my dad in the fields, she was raising chickens and selling eggs. She became a stringer for several newspapers, sending them personal items from our small community, and once she made the front page of the *Des Moines Tribune* with pictures and a story about a robbery and shooting in our town. In a few years, she had saved enough money to buy two large looms, and she wove rugs to order from rag strips the ladies brought in. Every church bazaar within miles featured the sturdy, colorful rugs from Claire's loom house, and my daughter still has and uses some to this day.

When Mom added shelves to her walls, she began filling them with novelty items she had made from wood, felt, cotton balls, fabric scraps, buttons, and whatever was handy. Whenever she ran across an idea for a new project, she rounded up supplies and had at least one made before she went to bed that night.

The making of her marble church took longer, I'm sure, as she framed it by gluing together nearly three hundred marbles and then installed a light and a music box in the center. This one was bright and beautiful after I finished cleaning it, but six marbles needed repair or replacement, and the light didn't work. I thought I might as well put it on one of the sale tables in the garage, although I doubted it would sell.

But, as it happened, right there on my countertop was a small blue bulb from the Christmas trimmings I was sorting for the sale. I screwed the bulb into place, plugged the cord into the wall, and the church came to glowing life. Ah, perhaps it would sell after all.

When I picked it up and started for the garage, my finger rested on the key that extended from the back wall of the church. It was the key that turned on the music box, which I had forgotten to test, and the church certainly wouldn't sell without that. So right there, in the back hallway, I sat down on the floor. I plugged the cord into the wall socket, wound the key, and was covered with chills as my little glass church sang, "I'll be loving you, always, with a love that's true, always. When the things you've planned need a helping hand I will understand, always, always. Things may not be fair always. That's when I'll be there, always. Not for just an hour, not for just a day, not for just a year, but always."

My mother has been gone for nineteen years, but for the moment she was right there with me, and I knew she had placed the music inside a church to remind me of her love and of God's love.

I didn't sell the church.

* * * * * *

Not then. But I did sell the church before the big move. By then I had relived all sentimental memories and narrowed my environment down to necessities. That's when my life became simpler, my direction more clarified.

The Communicator

At any moment, on a certain kind of late winter day, I find myself back in 1939 on a mountain of snow in Iowa, where a young girl shows me her world and inspires me again with the love she hoped I would never forget and horizons she hoped my voice would reach.

* * * * * *

Beverly and I were convinced we were in such attunement that we could communicate nonverbally from anywhere we happened to be, that we could surely read each other's thoughts. Had we not met on our very first day of school and ridden the school bus together all these years, shared our secrets, crowded our Saturdays and warm summer days with hiking and biking and overnight giggles?

Until we could practice and refine this mental telepathy, however, we planned to try communicating verbally across the two miles that separated our farm homes. We remembered a recent gray, foggy day when the air hung dense and humid and sounds of cows carried clear from the meadow. Surely our voices would carry as well, and we agreed to be on alert for such a day.

It came. We were almost buried in three days of heavy snow. Monster drifts tied the house to the barn in long, white ridges. The lane was closed, filled now with deep rolling sculptures, and no school bus came. Midafternoon the wind died down, and fog set in with a moving of warm air against the cold. A hint of spring was in the softness of its touch, yet the snow banks remained firm, packed now with a hard crust. The sky seemed close to earth, and sounds were hollow. It was a weird and wonderful day, exactly the kind we had waited for, and Bev would remember. I called her on the wall telephone (two shorts and a long), and we agreed upon four o'clock.

I bundled up, donned my snow pants and boots, took my Big Ben alarm clock, and climbed the enormous drift that filled much of the space between the house and the barn. The crest was blown smooth and flat, and I walked the length, testing its strength and looking for the highest spot with a clear shot for sound between the trees. From here I could look straight across to the roof of the barn. I could look downhill upon our house. I called out a few words. I gave a shriek, then a laugh, and they were magnified just as I had expected they would be. The stage was set, and conditions were perfect.

At exactly four o'clock, I cupped my hands and called out, "Yooooo … hoooooo." The fuzz from my mittens tickled my nose, and I sneezed. I took them off and called again. Was that a sound in return? Was it Bev, or was it my echo? Had we called at the same time? I put my mittens on and waited patiently for her to call to me, but there was silence, not even the sound of a dog barking or a cow mooing. I experimented then with yodeling sounds, and finally with words *are you there*?

Mom came out into the yard and shouted up to me, "What on earth are you doing?"

"I'm all right, Mom," I hollered back. "I'm communicating."

"Who are you communicating with?"

"Beverly."

"You just communicated with Beverly on the phone not more than half an hour ago. How about you come in the house and communicate with the dust cloth?"

"Yeah, Mom, in a minute," I said, and when she shut the door again, I thought to myself, *Oh, it is delicious, absolutely delicious up here all by myself.*

The colorless sky seemed to meld into the snow-covered ground below it. There was no horizon. Everything was covered with snow, so nothing stood out to catch my eye. It was just one big, soft, white, mushy world of wonderful feelings, and I began to sing.

"Little Sir Echo, how do you do? Yoo hoo. Yoo hoo." It was a song I had heard on the radio, and as I sang it now, my voice echoed back to me from all the buildings around ... the large, red barn, the machine shed, the grain bin, the chicken house, and of course the fringe of maple, oak, and walnut trees that framed the farm. It was like singing into a microphone from a large stage, and I imagined that the whole world was listening.

I went on to sing, "The music goes round and round, oh-oh, OH-oh, oh-oh, and it comes out here." I held my arms up as I paraded the length of that gigantic drift, and I fingered the notes with warm, little fingers inside my mittens. "Oh, you push that first valve down ... and the music goes round and round ... da-da-DAH-dah, da-dah, and it comes out here." I hit the DAH with a hoarse, throaty sound and a swish of my narrow hips.

It had begun to snow, quietly, moist flakes sticking to my eyelashes. Purple dusk set in and closed around me with the blanket of its awesome stillness. One yellow bulb glowed in the barn as the cows filed in for the evening milking, and I saw my dad, a pail in his hand, leaning in the doorway for a moment.

I stopped my prancing, stood on that mountain, and sang from my heart, for the world to hear, all the way through the songs that began "Tell me the story of Jesus, write on my heart every word," "On a hill far away stood an old rugged cross," and "I come to the garden alone while the dew is still on the roses" ("Ohhh, he walks with me and he talks with me, and he tells me I am his own"), and worked through to a patriotic finish with "My Country Tis of Thee," "Mine Eyes Have Seen the Glory" (even though I didn't know all the words), and finally, "Oh beautiful for spacious skies, for amber waves of grain." Lost in the echoes, my voice became a choir, and for what seemed like hours, I sang with myself, and "we" sang for the world. We sang all the love that I felt. My heart was swelled to bursting. Mom stepped out of the kitchen once, listened for a moment, then smiled and went back in.

I had forgotten about the dust cloth. I had forgotten about Beverly. But I had not forgotten about communicating. It was a good day for that.

Lovers of 1943

In the past few years, as the silver-haired Greatest Generation renews old friendships and speaks at last of memories from World War II, strange stories sometimes surface. Mine is a story that involves other people, so I must change their names to secure their privacy and hope they will not be offended if they happen upon this, recognize themselves, and read surprising news.

I was a student during the early forties in a college that came dangerously close to being a girls' school. One by one, the draft took our whole football team and most of the other guys we hung out with on campus and danced with on Saturday nights. We thought about them, wrote letters and sent packages to them, but we had no social life and were sometimes glad when we happened to meet a young airman from a neighboring airbase. These young men had volunteered or been drafted too and drawn away from their homes, their schools, and their plans for life.

I don't remember how I first met Marty Letcher. More than likely it was a blind date set up by one of his friends or one of my friends. We started going out. Not often, because I had a full class schedule and sometimes worked two or three part-time jobs.

"Going out" in the early forties meant that Marty called for me at the girls' dormitory, and we walked to the corner where he took my arm and gently helped me onto the creaking, rolling streetcar that delivered us to the downtown Orpheum theater. After the movie, we walked to a favorite restaurant for sandwiches and Cokes, then took the streetcar back to the campus where we often walked and talked, scuffling through autumn leaves or spring puddles. He was from the East Coast, I from the Midwest, but we were both thoughtful people who read a lot, and we had common interests.

One Saturday he called and said he must see me, as he wanted to have a serious talk. That night he told me he would not be calling me again. He said he was starting to care for me, but there was no future for us because he was Jewish and his parents would never accept me as his choice for a wife. He seemed very sad, but he was certain, and he was firm. He saw me back to the dorm, kissed me good-bye, and I never saw Marty again … except once.

Several months later, he called to invite me to his wedding. He had met a lovely girl named Helen Green. They had fallen in love, but best of all, she was Jewish, and his parents were delighted. He told me he first saw her and was drawn to her because she looked like me, and for some kind of young, sentimental reason, it was important to him that I be at his wedding.

I did go to the wedding in a downtown hotel, the first Jewish wedding I had ever attended, and I enjoyed meeting his bride and being included in the festivities.

The years have gone by so fast. I also married after the war, and I have lived a good life in the Midwest. I have kept in touch with my old college girl friends, but one in particular is close to me. Bev and I were childhood friends and went all the way through school together. Our husbands became friends also, and when we all retired, we often travelled to spend time together.

One weekend Bev and Dick were guests in our home. They had just returned from a reunion of his wartime military unit in a mountain retreat out west, and after dinner as we sat over glasses of wine, Bev said, "Oh, Dick, tell them that story about your friend."

"Yes," Dick said. "This guy Ray that I knew so well and worked with during the war told me that at one time he was stationed in that same town where you girls went to college."

Then he turned to Bev and said, "You know, I don't think I've told you this, but Ray told me he fell in love with a girl while he was there. Rather a sad story. The girl was Jewish and broke off the romance because she knew her parents would never accept him. He didn't know whatever happened to her and told me he often wonders."

"Bev," I said, "you know my past. Does this story not sound familiar? What a remarkable coincidence."

We both looked at Dick as I asked, "Did your Air Force friend happen to mention the girl's name? Maybe it's someone we know."

"He did," Dick replied. "Her name was Helen Green."

Bev and I looked at each other, drawing in a deep breath, and then said together, "And she married Marty Letcher!" We told our husbands the story of me and Marty.

There was silence for a moment as we each realized with chills that around our dining table we had just woven the final thread into a story that was sixty years old. We smiled in the candlelight and quietly raised our glasses to all the lovers of 1943.

No Albatross in Heaven

"I have a funny story to tell about my sister's death."
"You shouldn't make fun of the dead."
"Ah, but it was the dead having their fun with us."

It was still dark when the medics rolled the gurney out the back entrance, through the garage, and onto the ambulance, with me following. My daughter, Sara, hugged me good-bye at the door and said, "Take over." She had kept her promise to care for her Aunt Norma from the cancer diagnosis until death, and now she was physically and emotionally exhausted.

My sister's death had been imminent for days but had inched closer during the night with complications that put Norma beyond our care, even though Sara is a registered nurse and the wonderful Hospice aids and nurses had also been in and out to help. This morning, when the hospice nurse came after frantic calls at four o'clock, she ordered the ambulance, saying Norma needed to be in the hospital with an attending physician, and I elected to accompany her there.

The ambulance pulled out of the drive and headed for the freeway with me following in my car, deep breathing to stay alert and to keep from thinking. In the vehicle ahead of me, my sister was dying, or perhaps as her doctor later suggested, she had slipped out of that frail, sick body at the doorway and had died at home after all, as she had requested. Her last words to us were in sign language, her hand saying, "No … wait …"

But cancer doesn't wait.

My sister Norma was born when I was nine and was a complete surprise to me. I continued to be surprised by her because we were not much alike. In looks we were remarkably different, and we looked at life differently, forming diverse interests and even aligning ourselves with opposite causes and political parties. I raised children. Her love was animals. I was a dreamer, my head in the clouds; she was focused, calculating, and could beat me at almost any game. Winning was everything to her, especially at card games. I lacked the sports gene, but she loved sports and was a fan of the Green Bay Packers and the Wisconsin Badgers. Every fall she lived for those games, and she expected her teams to win.

We were always friends, and after we were both married, we and our husbands were friends together. Yet Norma, who never had children, formed an even closer friendship with my daughter, Sara, and through the years the two of them traveled back and forth some 1,300 miles to visit each other in their homes and to share interests. They went to football games. They had long telephone conversations. They delighted in playing jokes on each other, so when they were together, either one might be short-sheeted or find a plastic tarantula on her pillow or in her jar of night cream. Norma was a certified interpreter for the deaf, and she taught the American Sign Language to Sara so that they could communicate in any situation, which of course gave them further leeway for private jokes at family gatherings.

Our whole family had a love for Hawaii, and various ones of us, as we were able, planned winter vacations together in Honolulu. Evenings we would stroll out to meet local friends in places where musicians performed Hawaiian music and where every night became a party as talented guests were invited up to sing or to dance the hula. Most of them were Hawaiians, but Norma's husband, George, had an excellent voice and was often requested to sing. Norma was called up by various singers to interpret lyrics for the deaf, and many times people came up in tears to thank her and say they had never "heard" lyrics before. The "Hawaiian Lullaby" ("Where I live there are rainbows …") became a work of art with Norma's graceful interpretation.

Friends from the mainland sometimes joined us when they were in town, and we began to notice there was always one in the group who didn't fit. It was usually a tag-along. I remember the first one, a fellow teacher one of our friends thought might enjoy Hawaii but who didn't enjoy Hawaii, at least not its wonderful music, and who nodded off and was taking a nice nap when the club management asked us to remove her as her attitude was not good for their business. She was bored with the sights of Hawaii as well (if you can imagine that!), and we all began to call her (privately) "the albatross." Another year, friends who looked us up had brought along their mother, who was a lovely lady but a righteous evangelical who did not understand the medicinal value of a mai tai. We were kind to her, but, with a silent exchange of glances, we named her "the albatross."

Now it followed that Norma and Sara, with their constant kidding, should find appropriate times to begin dubbing each other "the albatross." Sara drew a crude picture of an albatross within a circle with a large slash mark indicating "no albatrosses allowed here" and posted it on her door when she knew Norma would be knocking. It may have started in Hawaii, but the albatross sign went home to Wisconsin with Norma and showed up on Sara's pillow the next time she visited there … and then to Texas with Sara, who placed it on the car seat the next time she picked up Norma at the airport.

The albatross sign began to show up in odd places. Sara was invited to a dinner in the home of friends from India, and the sign was on her chair at their dinner table. New neighbors moved next to Norma's lovely lakeside home in Wisconsin. She hadn't even met them yet, but one night her car lights picked up the albatross sign in their front window as she turned into her drive. On a Saturday in autumn, it showed up on her reserved seat in the Wisconsin stadium. Through the years, that sign traveled extensively and appeared in more and more surprising places, often with the secret help of friends.

Norma and Sara

Norma's husband, George, died in 1995, and her relationship with Sara strengthened. The next few years were the ones the two of them traveled together. In 2000, Norma and Sara joined our family in Hawaii, and we had a wonderful time sunning on the beach, touring the island, and joining friends for music on balmy, moonlit nights. But we noticed that Norma was a bit pale and distracted. The next month, she visited a doctor, who ordered tests and then surgery. She was found to have leiomyosarcoma, a rare and vicious cancer. The outlook was not good, and called for lengthy bouts of chemo and radiation.

Sara did not hesitate to offer her services. She went to Wisconsin and saw Norma through all the treatments, kept her comfortable and cared for, and took care of the house and all the details of daily living. In between trips to the doctor and the hospital, the two of them played Skipbo and other games and watched movies, with Norma's Himalayan cat, Lacey, snuggled between them on the sofa.

Their tomfoolery continued. One day Norma, with thinning hair and thinning body, sat in a recliner in a hospital treatment room receiving a long chemo drip, Sara by her side. When the nurse came in to check, she found they had reversed chairs, and both were wearing Groucho Marx glasses with big nose and mustache.

Sara had been in Wisconsin most of the time for almost two years. Her husband was understanding and often drove from Texas to Wisconsin to visit. I drove from Nebraska as well, to spell Sara from her care duties. Near the end, we called in Hospice. Those wonderful nurses, aides, and volunteers made the last few weeks bearable. Her pastor called often and was subjected to and caught up in the sense of humor that Norma and Sara still maintained. One evening, near the end, I said to Norma, who was by now completely bedridden, "Shall we get ready for bed now?" and she said, "Well, duh!"

When Sara, while cleaning Norma's dresser, discovered a beautiful piece of jewelry, a lapel pin shaped like a silver albatross in flight, she smiled and knew immediately what to do. It was already decided that Norma would be buried in her church choir robe, as she had been a strong alto and the choir librarian for many years and also because the robe would disguise the enormous weight loss. Sara took the albatross to the funeral home and asked the young junior director if he would pin it to the choir robe for the casket showing. It was a sad little act of love, the laying to rest of the albatross legend, but it was also an inside joke, the last move on their imaginary chessboard of tricks.

Lacey had become a concern. Norma could not find a home for Lacey that pleased her. People offered, but if they didn't love cats, they could not have Lacey, and if they already had a cat or a dog, she didn't want Lacey to play second fiddle. Norma loved cats as she loved people, and she wanted only the best for her pet. And so she lingered, no longer eating, and now away from every familiar routine except the comfort of stroking Lacey, nestled in the curve of her body.

Then suddenly Lacey showed signs of severe illness. Sara took her to the veterinarian, who diagnosed Lacey with cancer and said she must be put down immediately. It broke Norma's heart, and as she cried, two kind hospice nurses stayed by her side for hours, holding her to comfort her. The veterinarian told us he had seen it happen often, a pet passing on suddenly to show the way for its beloved master.

Now Norma was free, and she was leaving. That became at last clear to me as I followed the ambulance across town. Just as a bit of light broke through in the east, we turned onto manicured grounds and a long tree-lined driveway leading to the Don and Marilyn Anderson Hospice Center on the outskirts of Madison, one of the finest hospice facilities in the country. I parked and followed the gurney into the building, through wide, beautifully tiled hallways, past inviting, well-appointed parlors, and into the suite assigned to Norma. There she was put into bed as carefully and tenderly as a child, although her eyes were closed and she could not see the beautiful flower gardens outside her bay window.

The suite had every gracious accommodation for our comfort. I slipped a CD of her favorite music into the entertainment wall and placed by her bed an 8 x 10 picture of Norma at her prettiest, framed by a Hawaiian sunset. When the attending physician came in, he thanked me for doing this, with tears in his eyes, as he moved to examine the wasted body, now in deep coma.

Just a day and a night I was there with my sister and with the most warm and caring hospital staff imaginable. It was awful. It was wonderful. The worst was over. Separated now from her world of pain and from the demands of consciousness, Norma had only to "let go." By her bedside, holding her hand, I finally dozed, and the nurse woke me in the night to tell me she was gone.

In the days following, Sara and I did the usual things, visiting the funeral home and choosing the casket, making the arrangements for the service and ministry. Norma had selected the music, and we knew the choir members would outdo themselves to honor her. On the day of the funeral, they did, indeed, singing several of Norma's favorite anthems and ending with "Kanaka Wai' Wai" ("Let me Walk Through Paradise With You, Lord") and "Aloha 'Oe" ("Farewell to Thee").

We played taped Hawaiian music through the sound system before and after the service, sung by musical friends from Honolulu whose music she had enjoyed for over twenty-five years. An entire section of the church was reserved for the deaf, and an interpreter remained in front to sign the lyrics and the minister's words. When people were asked to share, one after another of her deaf friends came to the front to sign their moving memories of her service and friendship to them.

But these things were an anticlimax, a soothing and healing that followed our last surprising brush with the soul that was Norma. On the second day after her death, before the full family arrived, Sara and I were called to come and view Norma's body at the funeral home.

At the appointed hour, the young funeral director, who had shown us caskets two days before, met us at the door and ushered us into a long, narrow room with dim lights and soft green carpeting. Bowing slightly, he pointed toward the casket positioned at the end of the room and then stepped aside. We began the slow walk, the one we had dreaded for so long. We could see the open casket before us, and our knees were weak as we took the measured steps to see what we didn't want to see … Norma in still life, as we had never seen her.

Then, halfway there we stopped, and we both broke into laughter … loud, uncontrollable laughter that brought us to tears. At once both laughing and crying, we turned to the director with questions in our eyes, and he smiled and said, "She got you. She got you good." For there lay Norma's abandoned body in her satin-lined casket, and propped up in the quilted satin lid was the original crude sign with the picture of the forbidden albatross.

When we recovered, we asked the director how that sign had come to be placed there, and he told us it was brought in one day recently by a lady named Sue, and we realized this was Norma's Methodist minister.

We will never forget that day. It was my sister's most spectacular win ever.

Quiet Moments Heal

An evening by the fire
Is a cleansing of the soul,
A burning of the log
That was in my eye.

Fire fascinates.
It captures me and holds me
Helpless till I know its peace.
Flames leap up and go back down
To leap again in a different place.
I sit and stare, as part of it.
Thought is burned from my mind
Leaving it clean and dry.
Refreshed from the scourging,
I can feel again. I can see.

The fire burns low and crackles less,
But now I watch the blue
Around the edges of the flame.
The blue is like the music in the room.
It comes about the outside, encloses me,
And touches me inside.
It is the love that I was born with,
A fire that will never go out
Though it may leap up here, go down,
Leap up another place, another time,
Another way.

Sometimes I need to sit by it, alone,
This love of mine,
To warm and heal myself.

Some Things Last Forever

A great-grandmother remembers her grandparents

A child who spends time with a loving grandmother is blessed. A child who spends time with a loving grandmother and grandfather is doubly blessed … for life.

We lived in the country, and my grandparents lived in a small town in Iowa that had been home to both sides of my family since our ancestors arrived in the mid-1800s. "Staying over" with them gave me brief glimpses of town living, of focused morning activities and the leisurely afternoon pleasures of another generation.

They lived in the north end of town, across the street from the red brick public schoolhouse. He was a retired teacher and farmer and a long-term mayor of the town. My brother and I were invited to cross the street and have lunch with them every Friday, all through our school years, and I spent many weekends and summer days there.

It was a large, well-shaded, two-story house with a hip roof, a wraparound porch, gracious rooms, an open oak staircase with a banister for sliding, and a basement that was warm in winter with a coal-stoked, roaring furnace and cool in summer with hammocks and cots for sleep when the upstairs temperature soared. Of course they had a wonderful bathroom with a freestanding porcelain tub and hot and cold running water, which we did not yet have on the farm. They had a large, hedged lot with vegetable garden, flower garden, grape vines, plum, cherry, and apple trees with swings in them, and smooth sidewalks to skate on. How could a child not have fun in this place?

Although my Grandma Groves made special treats for us, most of her cooking was the quite ordinary fare preferred by older people. Bread and butter with jam, a bowl of potato soup, and a cookie with canned peaches would send my brother and me home raving about what we had eaten there, to my mother's amazement. But Grandma would say, "I made this just for you," and Granddad would ask us about school, about our friends, about what we saw and liked, what we wanted to do with our lives. After the meal, he would cut into thin slices a large caramel pecan candy bar he had won on a barbershop punch card.

In time spent with grandparents, a child's basic training about such things as honesty, fairness, neatness, duty, is often reinforced, even refined. Running a dust mop was presented as an opportunity, pulling weeds a privilege.

Somehow I think I might have procrastinated at home or tried to talk my way out of responsibilities. At my grandparents' I never did. Something in their eyes rewarded me every time I did the "right" thing. It was understood that they were always on my side. But more than that, because their life was slowed down, I was able to observe it more closely, and our timing was more in sync. They never hurried me. I took it all in.

Theirs was an orderly home. The morning was given to housecleaning, laundry, garden and lawn, shopping, maintenance. After lunch, Granddad wandered off to meet a crony for a chess game, or roamed the woods harvesting mushrooms for supper or hickory nuts for Grandma's delicious nut cakes. Grandma's afternoon was taken up with handwork. She sat in her sewing rocker in front of the picture window, and I pulled my little, round stool close. There we watched rain and rainbows, drifting snow, robins building their nests. There she taught me to embroider dishtowels, crochet doilies, and piece quilt blocks, as we listened to Ma Perkins, Helen Trent, or Pepper Young's Family on the dome-shaped radio.

But I wasn't just learning how to sew. I was learning that if I made a mistake, the whole thing would turn out crazy or crooked. I was learning patience, if I made a mistake to stop right then and take the stitches out. Start over. Get it going straight before it's too late. If it's worth doing, it's worth doing right.

I learned about relationships too. My parents had a good life and got along well, but they were both very busy, working hard morning to night. At my grandparents' home, I observed married life in a different way. I watched two people who had more time for each other than for anything else. Their concern was something to watch ... their teasing with pet nicknames, their spur-of-the-moment plans to go somewhere to explore or have fun, their contentment in the evenings drinking tea in their rockers by the radio, their love pats through the day, their thoughtfulness and small kindnesses, their soft tone of voice.

I clearly remember one summer day with them. We spent the morning pulling weeds in the garden, picking bright red tomatoes and green bell peppers. I was proud to be part of the harvest, although at home I would have considered it work. After lunch, Grandma baked and frosted small cakes in the shapes of diamonds, hearts, clubs, and spades. She let me wash the dishes. While things cooled, we walked through the rose garden, and we picked some pink roses, removed some of the petals, and set all to dry.

A few weeks later, she gave me a fine set of small china boutique jars filled with the rose petals and two tiny roses. "Keep this," she said. "They will dry completely, and then they will last forever."

The jars came from my favorite room in the house, the southeast corner room upstairs, with polished oak floors and wide windows that brought heavenly breezes through white lace curtains. When I was a child, Grandma put me there to nap on smooth, ironed sheets under her handmade quilts and then tiptoed out after putting a Fritz Krietzler record on the Edison. Later in life I would go there in my mind to fall asleep in the peace of that household.

As a high school and college student, I still treasured time spent with my grandparents, and before my wedding, my friends gathered and helped me dress in that same guest bedroom. One day, a year after my wedding, I came to visit Grandma Groves, and she had something for me.

Again in that same bedroom, she took from a dresser drawer two long, coiled plaits of beautiful, auburn hair. "This is my own hair that was bobbed in 1926 when you were just a baby," she said. "I want you to have it because it's about the color of yours, and you may want to have hair pieces made one day."

How fast time flies. When I was facing the changes that come late in our lives and going over all my treasures to decide which to keep, I opened a dresser drawer and came upon a rolled-up newspaper from 1949. I unrolled it, and the two coils of Grandma's hair that spilled out were as shiny and bright as they were on the day that they were cut. And nearby, on the dresser still sat my small china jars. I removed a lid, and there were the petals I'd picked in my grandmother's garden. They still had the scent of roses!

It wasn't until days later, standing in front of the mirror brushing my own silver hair, that I flashed on something. My grandmother's hair was tucked away in a drawer for eighty years, and it had never changed color! It had never turned gray! Captured young and put away in a safe place, it stayed young, it stayed perfect, just like my memories of that time and place, those wonderful grandparents, and all the lessons I learned from them.

Turn About

So many things are left unsaid when the subject of aging comes up. Whether we are the old one or a relative of the suddenly old one, we don't like to think or talk about the problems or the changes we notice.

Like the old one forgets names and where he puts things. Of course. Like the old one has a runny nose. Typical. Like the old one often hurries to the bathroom, and lucky sometimes if he makes it. Yes. Like the old one wakes up in the middle of the night and falls asleep in the middle of the day. Just like his grandpa did.

But have you noticed here a common thread? If you are a parent or even a sibling, you must realize this is the way of newborns. They have runny noses, they have innocent bladders, they sleep when sleep comes upon them. So now you have a closer understanding of our comings and our goings.

I would consider it a privilege to release life slowly, going out gently as I came in, glad to not be one of those who left suddenly and often unprepared, although this may have been right for them. Lingering, I have time to regroup, to gather all of my pictures and sort them for the children … or for the wastebasket. (Who wants a picture of a mountain I saw once in Montana?)

I have time to enjoy all the grandchildren and great-grandchildren without feeling the slightest bit of responsibility. I can see their challenges, their talents, their possibilities, and just hope it leads to a wonderful life. I won't be here to see it. But then my grandparents weren't here to see my entire life either, and I'd like to think I'd have made them proud.

I sometimes set the timer to suggest when I should go. Not when I must but when I can. I keep an appointment calendar and also notes on the refrigerator to remind me where to be and when. I call old friends to check on them, and I keep in close touch with all my family. I walk carefully about the house and use the handrails by the steps and in the bathroom. I wear a pendant to enable me to call for help if I should fall or feel sick. Not that I'm ill or crippled or frail. No, not at all. In fact, I am healthy and very active. I do these things to please the kids.

Just as those very adult children once cautiously pulled themselves up in the crib, carefully circled the playpen, took their first steps with help, and hung on to the railings while they conquered the stairs. Of course. They did it to please their parents.

Revolving Door

The opposite of growing up
is growing down,
losing stature inch by inch,
losing teeth (without the fairy),
going back to timeless days of
reading clouds and doing as I please,
back to runny noses, comfort food
and little naps, people smiling
when they see me, glad to feel
that they're still young;
and if I suffer inconvenient pains
on my way out, I will remember
how I battled mumps and
measles coming in, and though
I dread the infant days that lie ahead,
I bear the thought, remembering
what was there for me on entry
will be there for me on exit,
and that thing is love.

BELIEVING

Thunderburst

I never fear the thunder
Or the lightning,
Never run and hide,
But here, behind my curtains,
Safe and glad to be inside,
I feel the sky,
Roll with the clouds
That groan and grumble by,
Grow tense with pleasure and with pain
At every streak of energy that shocks
Before the rain.

Then, when the water's driving hard
Against the glass,
I feel the cleansing sheet
Of power pass;
I shiver slightly at the chill
And know when nature's
At the bursting point …
It will.

How fresh things then appear,
How clear to see
In that brief shining moment
When the sun breaks forth for me
And I am warm,
The thirsty spirit, growing dry,
And never really knowing why,
Asks for a raindrop
And is purified by storm.

Meditation

Somewhere in my mind
And in my heart,
A deep and private place
I go to be apart
From man and selfish care,
There is a quiet shelter
And a friend who meets me there.

Childlike, on the borderland
Of sleep, when I release
The rigid image that I keep
For all the world to see,
I step into my garden
With another, greater me.

Strange and sweetly awesome,
Yet so right that I should walk
And talk with Him into the night
Or find Him waiting when I wake
Or, sometimes, when I'm gazing
At a sunset or a lake.

We talk about my lessons
And review
The things I planned to do with life
And didn't do;
We look together at my deeds,
Encourage growing seedlings,
Sprinkle hope, and pull the weeds.

We share the dream of life,
To learn and grow.
In spirit's love, we think,
We plan, we feel, and know,
Though none can sense or see
The lovely roses in my garden
But the Christ within and me.

Afterglow

Through the kitchen window
I watched the sun go down
And cast its rosy shadow
On the western edge of town.
It streaked the sky with lavender
Then winked a golden eye
Before it slipped in silence
From a purple-painted sky.
And I thought for just a moment
In the softly fading light,
Now wasn't that a lovely way
For God to say goodnight?

Abundance

Fortune often smiles upon
The ones who court her least,
The ones who never buy their bread
But daily set their yeast
    Aside to rise.

Abundance to the faithful
Seldom comes as a surprise.

Forever

The trouble with our concept of forever
    Is our inability to see
        A picture not developed yet
          Of what we'd hoped to be,
A never-knowing feeling
    For events yet to occur
        Through dim yet present memories
          Of what we always were.

Goodnight from an Autumn Oak

Enough of growing!
Let me rest and gather strength.
Here I undress and, sighing,
Stretch full length
To fast and meditate.
Here, see my naked limbs full view,
The errant ones and those that grew,
This season, tall and straight.

No matter in my age I am
Less perfect. Heaven knows!
Perhaps a crooked place was made
To furnish younger neighbors' shade
Or form branch offices
For squirrels or for crows.

Now, turning toward the light,
I give my consciousness to night.
A time for everything.
A time to sleep and
Dream my spring.

The Gate

I don't remember how I got here or what the entire plan was. But it was arranged for people to meet me at the gate and, you know, fill me in on how to act, what to say and not say, and how things are done in this place.

I lived with them for a while, and they showed by example how to have a good life here, as well as sharing the rules that would keep me out of trouble. They were good people.

In a few years, they were gone but I found new friends, and in time I had a mate and children of my own ...

Wait ... wait ... they are not my own, never were. I remember now. They are the ones I was sent to meet at the gate.

Heirlooms in the Attic (A Look at Spiritual Genealogy)

Out of the blue comes a letter from a distant relative I've never heard of. Her name is Eileen. She lives in Virginia and is seeking information concerning a common ancestor, one Edward McClung who drowned in the Kanawha River in 1792.

I sigh and head for the basement to consult the archives of a past life, a time when I too wondered who I was and where I came from. Somewhere I have files with dates and names that others helped me to compile. I was glad for their help and am glad now to help Eileen.

I will type them up nicely, all the facts I have, and send them with love, but here is a letter I would like to send.

Dear Eileen,

So something is stirring. You are beginning to wonder who you are. That is good.

Some years ago, I wondered about myself, my history, and I went through the process you are going through now. It's a mind-blower, isn't it? First you have two parents, then four grandparents, then eight great-grandparents, then sixteen, thirty-two, sixty-four, 128! When will it end, you ask, as you accumulate birth and death certificates, county and church records, census files, pictures, letters, books. Does the heritage go all the way to the beginnings of time?

In your search, you are sure to find lots of respectable farmers, a few ministers, clerks, or horse thieves and most with a series of wives (for women died young and had to be replaced). Over and over you will find the names John, Edward, Elizabeth, and Sarah. If you have children, you may have named them John, Edward, Elizabeth, or Sara … at least for a middle name. You will wonder what they have in common with the originals. You will wonder what all this has to do with you.

I did too. One night, I sat up late puzzling over this burdensome file I'd put together. It was becoming such hard work that I suddenly became honest with myself. Why was I doing all this?

It occurred to me quite spontaneously that if I traced the record back far enough, I would find myself in some way related to everyone on earth! Can you imagine the stunning effect of that insight? All of us one big family, interspersing and trading genes and attitudes so that we can learn together, leveling out and refining our understanding through this experience?

I have a feeling we could learn a lot by comparing notes, Eileen, but maybe not in the way you think. Why do you suppose we were born into those families and those situations? What did we have to learn from it? Do you have any idea how many different family patterns you and I have been exposed to through our genes? What a rounded experience we have had!

Most of what we are today is a result of that intermingling. Our opinions, attitudes, prejudices, habits, ways of thinking and responding to life were handed down to us by our parents, who got them from their parents, and so on.

Down to us came the feelings of the ancestor who was a landowner and the feelings of one who was a serf, one who was a factory owner and one who was a file clerk, one who was a judge and one who was a horse thief. And we wonder why there is confusion in the attic.

Actually, I'd like to think that's not what they really were and that, deep down, they knew it. They were playing a cosmic game to see what they could learn from it. And just like little boys who play cowboys and Indians or cops and robbers, they went home at night and laughed together, planning which roles to take tomorrow.

The toys they used in their games and the tools they used in their trades are of little value in this age. The devices they used to shield their true natures in difficult times of survival are equally antiquated. We have survived, and now we want to succeed.

Sorting out my spiritual genealogy means looking at the concepts I hold and deciding whether to keep Grandfather's Irish temper, Grandmother's "suffering syndrome," Aunt Sally's stuffy pride, Father's anger. It's seeing that the size of the family nose or the family bank account is not so important as the size of the heart or the size of one's self-respect.

Hand-me-down concepts are just like other antiques. Some are priceless, and some are junk.

On the rainy days of our lives, we go to that attic and begin to throw out the rusty relics of fear, anxiety, and resentment, feelings of being greater or lesser than others, of being manipulated or controlled. We dig through to the source and at the bottom of the heap, safely preserved through the centuries, we find the precious treasures of love, trust, patience, hope, and understanding, which were ours from the start, our true inheritance.

We meet here briefly, Eileen, through the mail, as distant cousins, but think and remember, and you will know we were always sisters.

Much love,
DJM

Note: The above piece was written in 1982, when tracing family history really was an expensive and full-time job. Today the Internet has made the search quicker, simpler, and more fun. And now science is making it possible to search our family's medical history. Tracing one's spiritual history, however, may be a matter of discerning what is the "real me" and what are the ghosts of my ancestors.

Growing Pains and Pleasures

There was a time a few decades ago when our climate began to change. Not the weather but something within us. It was so subtle that most people missed it, except those who were restless, exploring, seeking something, not even knowing what. For me, it meant asking questions, following hunches, noticing book titles and upcoming lectures or workshops having to do with awareness, change, growth. It was a feeling as if I had outgrown my clothes and needed a new set, and I went looking. I was not alone.

Some people turned to yoga and eastern meditation, seeking peace and understanding. Programs of all sorts sprang up in those years, anything from EST (Erhard Seminar Training) to weird cults, to expanded and experimental church programs, to truly helpful spiritual growth programs. I was fortunate to find one of the latter and had a most wonderful experience over a period of years learning to understand my two natures, the intellectual part of me and the feeling nature, and how to find a balance between the two, leading to harmony and purpose in my life.

About the same time, for fun, I drove a hundred miles to visit a psychic who was recommended to me. Not that I believe in psychics or disbelieve in psychics, but it was something I wanted to experience. She was an elderly lady who laid out her ordinary playing cards as a focal point and then began to tell me what she saw. For one thing, she told me my son-in-law was in the service. I said no he was not in the service. She said she believed he was in the Air Force, but, oddly, she saw him wearing an army uniform. She also told me that the state of Hawaii would be very important to me for most of my life. *Ha*, I thought, *she is a fake. I know nothing about Hawaii, have never been there, nor planned to go, and my son-in-law is not in the service.*

When I arrived home from that session, my son-in-law was standing in our driveway washing his car. He and my daughter had come for a visit.

He was wearing an old army shirt he had bought in a used clothing store. At the dinner table, he broke the news that he had just enlisted in the US Air Force.

I became a believer … not in psychics, but in the fact that sometimes when we start to ask questions, we start to get answers, and maybe we just need a little proof to show it's okay to explore.

Shortly after that, to my surprise, my husband and I had the opportunity to visit Hawaii with a business group. That was in 1975. We fell in love with the islands, of course, as most do. The next year, we returned with our son Tom, the last of the brood, and we explored further, loving more. In 1978, we bought a small place of our own in Honolulu and established a foothold on paradise, a decision we would never regret. We vacationed in Honolulu every year when snow hit the Midwest and temperatures dropped below zero.

We made friends there, had our own favorite haunts and adventures, felt a part of the local scene, and most of the time were comfortably recognized as Kamaaina (literally meaning child of the land, used for a long-term resident of Hawaii).

In the early years, we noticed the distinct difference between island time and mainland time, in ways having nothing to do with Greenwich or Atomic time. Mainlanders seem always to be in a hurry. Hawaiians take their time. We noticed how the Hawaiian residents move and speak … so relaxed, so pleasant. We made friends with local musicians, and they taught us about Hawaiian music, and while we couldn't sing all the words to all the songs, we knew the feelings of every song in our hearts and felt what Hawaiians feel in those first few bars of their favorite songs and when at the end of the song they shout "hauna hou" (sing it again!). We stood in a circle at the end of an evening, holding hands, and sang together in harmony the Hawaii state song ("Hawai'i Pono'i") and one of the US patriotic songs, sometimes also a Hawaiian lullaby. There was such a feeling of oneness it bought tears.

Well, it was our feelings we came to Hawaii to discover, though we didn't know it in the beginning. It is in our feelings that we experience inspiration. It is in our intellect that we plan and carry out that inspiration and give it direction. Finding a balance where the two work together is the foothold of peace and a lifetime goal.

In those early years, we attended a few evenings in one of Hawaii's nice hotels where a Dr. Richard Ireland appeared to discuss psychic experience. He was amazing. He could select people at random and give them their social security numbers. That was an attention getter, and then he answered questions sent up to him. In addition to very helpful answers, he was often able to tell people where they lived, how many children they have, and surprising details about their lives. He was always right.

Once he singled me out and had me stand. He said, "You are also psychic. Do you know that?"

I answered, "Yes, but only because I think everyone is psychic."

"You are exactly right," he said, and explained that his appearances were to serve no purpose except to help people understand that.

One more memory from my psychic reading mentioned earlier. The lady told me I would one day become the matriarch of my family. I didn't understand that at the time, but now I do. I attended the funerals of my father, mother, brother, sister, brother-in-law, one great-grandparent, four grandparents, and all my aunts and uncles. And finally, my husband. I am the only one left from those generations. Now I am not the wisest but certainly the oldest one in the family, as was forecast.

I am still seeing positive signs of a step we all took rather naturally in recent years, without conscious awareness, in acknowledging our feeling nature. If you are middle aged or older, you will remember when hugs were scarce and more likely to be a duty than a pleasure. Now we hug on meeting and on saying good-bye. We hug for support, for sympathy, for joy. We hug old friends and greet new friends with hugs. On introduction, we sometimes hug strangers. We share love with hugs and no longer feel awkward or self-conscious about it. It is a good step.

A Brief History of Hugs (or From Handshakes to Hugs)

A hug is one of the most beautiful ways I know to experience another person. A hug is one of the most beautiful ways I know to experience myself. A hug is a greeting, a balancing, a healing, a blessing. A hug is a reminder that we are not alone. It asks nothing. It takes nothing away. It gives to both alike. A hug feels good.

We have not always hugged. Well, yes, there were the Hollywood hugs and the duty hugs, but I'm talking soul hugs, the way people so often instinctively come together these days to exchange an honest moment of people love and acknowledgment.

Speaking for myself, I have not always been a hugger, because I grew up in a community where people did more talking than touching. In the rather cool Scandinavian environment of an earlier rural Midwest, children were coddled and caressed until the age of reason. Then they were graduated to handshakes and, at most, cheek pecks.

When I married, I did hug my husband, of course, because he was privileged, and we had a contract to hug. I had a contract on my children too, if you know what I mean. They were sweet, they were cute, and they were mine. I loved them in every way possible until their teeth fell out and they made Brownies or the baseball team. Then I fearfully turned them over to the world and guided them with my head so that my heart would not get in the way.

But a subtle light began to dawn. Was it in the seventies or was it in the eighties? New stirrings prompted me to read new books, seek new friends, discover meditation, take yoga lessons, attend lectures and sharing groups. I was reaching, and I was becoming more reachable. Before I knew what had happened, someone had hugged me soundly, impersonally, and unconditionally. I learned how to pass it on and feel good about it. I began to look for opportunities to give and receive hugs, taking them naturally as the spirit moved me and others.

Through the years, I did indeed become a very comfortable hugger. You want to know about hugs, ask me. I won't tell you, I'll show you. Although I love words, I have found that hugs creep into spaces that words never penetrate. Hugs make words unnecessary. Hugs find the heart and say, "You're okay." Hugs hum, and the humming is the harmony of the universe.

As I rediscovered my feelings, life became more spontaneous. I began to hug my children again, the oldest of whom had not felt my touch in a while. The youngest one scarcely missed a hug, and one day when he was twelve, he brought a friend into our home and blatantly hugged me in his presence, saying, "See! I do too hug my mother!" The neighbor kid rolled his eyes in yucky disbelief but returned later to witness a second demonstration for proof.

I began to hug my mother, my brother and sister, and, surprisingly, they responded. I was sorry I had not hugged my father before he died. Now family reunions took a new turn, and eventually, for the first time, I saw fathers abandon the traditional handshake and throw their arms around their grown sons. Little did I know that in just a few years, athletes would hug at the end of the game, presidents would give a hug along with a medal, television hosts would greet their guests with hugs. Everyone responds to a loving, impersonal hug once he has experienced it, and old customs can change in a flash.

Impersonal is a key word. When I share my energy asking something in return, the huggee responds by tightening up, sensing that I am out to control him. He may take offense because he feels my insincerity. When I am Me (the soul Me), giving without thought of reward or entanglement, everyone relaxes. They take the love I have to give, and that love is doubled as it flows back through me.

The perfect hug—well it doesn't have to be perfect, but I am speaking of a satisfying hug—is not a strong grasping and holding or squeezing, nor is it wishy-washy like the handshake of a halfhearted greeter. The good hug meets you halfway and does not intrude. It spreads warmth to relax you. It holds you for a moment of absolute peace and brings the same response from the other party, for you meet in your feelings, where trust is mutual.

A good hug is medicine of the gods. It can guide and nourish the spirit, healing the hurts of our learning experience. It speaks in every language, crosses barriers of religion, culture, breeding, and age. It recognizes and salutes the precious moment, helps us share with others both our happiness and our grief. Hugs in airports and churches send our loved ones into new adventures … trips, marriages, wars. Hugs welcome our loved ones, and even strangers, home.

But we have not always hugged. Thank heavens for the wonderful seventies (or was it the eighties?) when hugs were catching, when waves of a more certain, more relaxed culture were sweeping across the country. Looking back, it seems to me that almost overnight hugs caught on. If I talk to someone now who has never experienced life without hugs, I can know that he/she is younger than forty … or is Hawaiian! Hawaiians hug from the heart and always have. That's what Aloha is all about.

I remember once when my three-year-old grandson Jason, visiting from Chicago, sat at my kitchen table, chin on fist, and pondered, "Grandma, do you know where God is?"

"Well, let me think a bit," I said, and took him into my lap. He leaned against me, and his arm stole around me in a comfortable hug. I tightened my arms in a loving gesture and asked him to tell me about God.

"Well, I know where God is," he said, pointing to his chest. "God is right inside these walls." I hugged him again and was sure he was right.

Hugs and true feelings shared tell us more about the divine experience than any book ever written. Children know this. Open in their feelings and their intuition, they show us where we can be if we allow our souls to lead.

When our youngest son was about eighteen months old, we took him with us to a dinner club. Far across the room was another couple with a baby daughter. The two youngsters had never met, yet they recognized and toddled toward each other, arms outstretched, shouting, "Baby!" They fell into each other's arms and embraced with such joy and pure love it made chills run down the spine of everyone in the room.

A good hug is recognition of another soul. We are, after all, brothers and sisters on the same planet out of all the universe.

The Good Hug

The good hug
Draws you gently
Into light,
Asking nothing but
Time out for peace.
It does not intrude
But meets halfway,
Touching softly,
Spreading love as
Butter on warm toast.
The giving and the taking
Flow both ways to smooth
The rough spots of the aura
As the good hug
Brings two souls
Not face to face,
But heart to heart.

The world needs time out for peace.
Hug someone and pass it on.

—Doris Markland

Lifting the Old Rugged Cross

Sometime in the early seventies, my then minister called me and asked for my help. He said "The Old Rugged Cross" was such a favorite of his parishioners, but the words of the song were so sad and depressing they did not make the Sundays very sunny, and actually often detracted from his positive message. He asked if I would write new words to sing with this traditional melody, as an experiment.

New words for "The Old Rugged Cross"? Well, I thought, that would indeed take some nerve. But he said it was just for a trial, so I set about letting new words go through my mind as I went about my housework that morning.

By midafternoon it had come together, and as I sang it over and over, fine-tuning, I felt that it was fine-tuning me as well. No longer the feelings of suffering and sorrow and shame, no longer the memories of the sad funerals of my parents and grandparents. Even the tune sounded different with powerful words of strength instead of despair.

I sent it off to the minister, and I must tell you that he never responded in any way. No thanks. Not even a phone call. So I must assume he was shocked by my renovation and never tried the lyrics on his congregation.

Still, I will share these words and will ask one small favor of you. Just for me, would you pick up your book and sing them, please? See how you feel.

The New Rugged Cross

There's a new world of thought
In the truth Jesus taught,
There's a new world of living for me
When the way that I choose
Transforms and renews
And lifts me to all I can be.

Chorus: So I'll walk in the light of his truth,
Turn from suffering and sorrow and sin
To the joy and the sunshine of youth
That live in my kingdom within.

There's a new world of love
When my thoughts rise above
All that's human and petty and low,
For the good that I see
Is the love within me
That shines on the world that I know.

Chorus: So I'll walk in the light of his truth,
Turn from suffering and sorrow and sin
To the joy and the sunshine of youth
That live in my kingdom within.

There's a new world for me
For my spirit is free,
Though in flesh, yet a part of the Word
When I know that I am
And I shall be again
And forever a child of the Lord.

Chorus: So I'll walk in the light of his truth,
Turn from suffering and sorrow and sin
To the joy and the sunshine of youth
That live in my kingdom within.

They Did It Their Way

Looking back, I realize it was probably strange that my friend Donna and I so often had conversations about death. Maybe it was because our parents were old and ailing. I remember sitting over coffee with our husbands, having a long debate about cremation. Donna and I thought it was practical; the men thought it was weird.

"Bury me any way you want," my husband said, "but just be sure that at my funeral someone sings 'I Did It My Way.'"

"That's perfect," Donna said. "That's what I want for my funeral too, a real Sinatra version of 'I Did It My Way.'"

It would suit her, I thought, for Donna was really unique. A thoughtful, caring person, she was always helping others. She lived rather than talked her religion. She was open and honest with her feelings and lived by her own standards, avoiding many of the games that humans play.

When she died tragically at a young middle age, her death came as a result of her efforts to help another person, and it was sudden. Her husband arranged for a public memorial service at the church but asked me to join the family for a private viewing earlier at the funeral home.

We met there on a warm summer morning, Donna's family and me, all of us still in shock. I stood for a long time in the lobby of the funeral home listening to the soft classical and religious music that came through the speaker system. Donna's family was with her body, and I did not want to intrude. When the minister took them into another room for prayer, I walked into the viewing room and found myself alone with the body of my good friend and perhaps with her spirit as well.

Donna's body lay in a plain wooden box draped with satin, for her husband had, after all, arranged for her cremation. It was a simplicity she would have appreciated.

As I stood there looking at her dear familiar face, I was flooded with memories of all the good times we'd had and the long talks over many years as we each sought meaning in our lives. Organ music numbed the pain and cushioned the embarrassment of this surprising meeting.

Donna seemed nearby, and I began talking mentally to her, thanking her for her friendship. The mood seemed light. I felt her smiling, almost laughing, at the ridiculous drama in which we found ourselves taking part.

I remembered a long, rainy afternoon we had spent recently in deep conversation, and how as we said good-bye she took my hand and said, "If I had as many friends as I have fingers on this hand, you would be one of them." And then she leaned over and kissed my cheek, something she had never done. It stuck with me.

Now, suddenly, the music changed and "The Old Rugged Cross" gave way to the standard popular recording of "I Did It My Way." It was the Chairman of the Board himself, old Blue-Eyes come for Donna's funeral. As unlikely and impossible as this sounds, it happened. In a moment out of time, I touched Donna's hand and listened to the song from beginning to end, covered with chills and with feelings of freedom and happiness.

When the sound system returned to normal funeral music, I left the room to be with the family. I didn't tell them what I had experienced. Who would believe me? The funeral director said the song was not on their playlist.

Some time later, I had occasion to visit with a very wise spiritual mentor, and I told him the story. He was not surprised. "It was her birthday," he said. "She could request anything she wanted."

Postscript:

In 2011, my husband, Gene, died. We had a church funeral. An old childhood friend, now a minister, conducted the service, and then our sons and several friends rose to relate interesting and funny stories about Gene and how he did things well and in his own way. After the closing prayer, the pallbearers, his sons and grandsons, surrounded the casket, and as they took their first steps, Sinatra's soft, tender version of "I Did It My Way" filled the church. Our children had seen to that. No one thought it strange. It seemed so right for Gene.

Precipice

One night early in the 1980s, I awoke, went to the kitchen table, sat down with a tablet and pencil and wrote these words without a pause. It was as if the pencil wrote them. I put the words into a drawer, went back to bed, and fell into a deep sleep.

For a time I kept them to myself, and then I dared to show them to a few individuals. Each of them reacted in a different way, but all in a positive way, as if the words were written just for them and carried a message meant for them. I think it almost frightened me, and I put the piece away. Recently I found it again, and I'm sharing it here for whatever it means to you.

I had been running for as long as I could remember. If I knew, I had forgotten what I was running from and, more to the point, what I was running to.

Running had become a way of life. It was something to do, and it certainly kept me busy. Other runners joined me now and then for a stretch and then peeled off in their own direction … or dropped, exhausted, seeing we were going nowhere. It was a lonely business, running day and night, but somehow comfortable.

My body had shaped itself into the constant poise of the mechanics … back straight, hips taut, chin into the wind. My legs and feet no longer ached but tingled numbly on every impact, a concrete reminder regular as a clock beat, to keep me asleep on the run.

I could have gone on forever had the earth not ended. Looking out, I saw nothing before me but space. My toes, coming to the last inch of ground, dug in and prayed for balance while my frame convulsed against dead air and loss of motion.

Swaying there on the edge, my legs jerking and trembling to hold me back, I saw below me nothing but water. Far below this sudden cliff, there was nothing but deep, blue water everywhere, without another shore in sight.

There was no solution. I could not retreat because I dared not lift a leg to take that one step backward. To pitch forward was the natural thing to do, and any movement I initiated would pitch me forward to my almost certain death.

It was a split second that lasted a thousand years. Through my mind raced scenes and memories … running, running through the history of my soul.

It was a moment to meet my maker, and meet my maker I did. In every scene, I saw and felt and knew and understood, at last, the one who had created it. I knew, and now I could no longer run. I knew, and still I could not move.

"Help me!" I called to the wind and the Wise Ones. "Help me, oh help me! I want to live!" And with a force both gentle and swift, the Wise Ones came, encircled me with loving arms—and pushed.

The Twenty-Third Psalm through My Eyes

A friend asked me if I could explain the Twenty-Third Psalm to her, and I gave her question some thought, wondering what the psalm meant to me. I realized that while I had always found this psalm very comforting, some of the phrasing had puzzled me too. So I took a week and meditated each day on a different part of it, asking my guidance to help me clarify what the words mean to me at this time. This was my insight:

The Lord is my shepherd. I shall not want.

I have a connection to the Holy Spirit that helps me to fulfill my needs.

He maketh me to lie down in green pastures.

As shepherds take their herds to where the grass is green and there they make their home, their resting place, so Spirit leads me to where my spiritual food is abundant and then moves me on, in time, to even greener pastures as I grow.

He leadeth me beside the still waters. He restoreth my soul.

The energy of Spirit flows like water, and pools when it is not used. Flowing with Spirit keeps me on the right path for me, and when I pause to reflect and regroup, I am always near the deep clear pool of energy and wisdom.

He leadeth me in the paths of righteousness for his name's sake.

When I am relaxed, focused, and in tune with Spirit, I move through life with confidence, avoiding pitfalls, going in directions that feel right according to my unique thrust, as promised.

Yea, though I walk through the valley of the shadow of death I will fear no evil, for thou art with me. Thy rod and thy staff they comfort me.

Death of the body is inevitable and always a possibility at any time, but I do not live in fear that it will come upon me out of season or be brought upon me by another, for I lead a life of purpose and have the comfort of knowing that my guidance is near and available to keep me in the right place at the right time … if I will only listen.

Thou preparest a table before me in the presence of my enemies. Thou anointest my head with oil. My cup runneth over.

My spiritual connection is highly personal. It is something that takes place within me and is unknown to those around me, so that even in a hostile environment, my communication is clear, unchallenged, and fulfilling. With insight through my gifts, I am constantly nourished and blessed by Spirit.

Surely goodness and mercy shall follow me all the days of my life and I will dwell in the House of the Lord forever.

Openness to Spirit is openness to love and to the good feelings and the good life that love promotes and extends, for the life of the soul never ends, and those who understand this choose to live in love and will do so forever.

The Last Christmas

One by one our families came for that last Christmas together, driving over the river and through the woods, finally up the long, snowy lane to home. The old farmhouse, where my father was born and where my brother and sister and I were all born, never changed. It was there for us, its windows pouring light onto the snow through wreaths and candle decorations, and the back door opening at once to a barrage of stomping feet, of hugs and kids and presents for the tree.

We knew from the beginning that it would be an extraordinary holiday. Our dad had fought the good fight, going through seven major surgeries, chemo, and radiation, in attempts to still the cancer. But the cancer was winning and now, just home again from the hospital but home for good, Dad welcomed us, looking thin and pale but oh so happy to see us.

We did the things we used to do, and Christmas Eve we were all in church, filling two pews. Dad had been president of the church board forever and had given the annual lay sermon for years. Now the congregation felt our pain and held us up through that last Christmas service.

Back home, Mom served us oyster soup and salads and Christmas cookies, and then we all gathered in the "parlor" (as it had been called in its early days) to sing carols around the organ and then to take our places for the Christmas exchange, adults on the sofas and chairs, and kids at their feet. Two of the youngest were assigned to deliver presents to Granddad, who cut the string and announced who it was from and who they were to deliver it to. We all watched as each gift was opened and acknowledged.

When the gifts had been distributed, my dad cleared his throat, asked for our attention, and said he had some words he would like to say to us. A hush fell on the room, and we made every effort to give our full attention and not to reach for tissues.

"I had hoped to have a gift for each of you," he said, "but I have had no opportunity to go shopping. However, I have looked about, and in my dresser drawer I found these wonderful expensive billfolds you all have given me through the years, and there is one here for each of the men." This brought smiles as the billfolds were passed around.

"Now," he said, "I am so disappointed not to have something unique to give each and every one of you. But I will give you the only thing I have to give."

He smiled at each of us as he continued, "In the long nights when I have been ill and unable to sleep, I have thought and thought about what I might have for your Christmas, and it finally came down to this, a story for you to remember when you think of me.

"I want you to picture this: when I was a child, this town was new. We did not have paved streets. Right through the town were dirt roads, and in times of bad weather, they developed deep ruts. There were no sidewalks either, only paths, and at times they also had puddles and ruts of mud. As a small boy, when we came to town, I walked along with my father, a tall man, and I did my best to keep up with him. But it was hard. Once in a while, there would be a commotion. A horse would balk and shinny, rear up and threaten to run amuck with carriage and all. In times like these, I would reach up and grab my father's hand, and he would guide, lifting and swinging me over the rough parts, keeping me by his side.

"This picture came to me one night as I lay awake, and I realized that is exactly what I am doing now. I want you to know that I have an enormous sense of peace and the knowledge that my heavenly father is beside me through every hour. He has taken my hand and guided me through this whole thing, even the long and lonely nights. I realize that his hand has been there all along, and at any time I could have reached up and taken it to guide me in life. I want you to know that his hand is there, always, for you."

It was indeed a present. It was enough. I never forgot it. I never think of Christmas or of my father without remembering his story.

Soul Survivor

Do you ever wonder what old people think about aging … and death? Have you ever asked? In this trilogy, a great-grandmother, the last leaf on her family tree, gives a glimpse into her mind and her heart on the subject of aging and death.

Senior Citizens

When I graduated the first time, and I mean when I graduated from high school, it was one of the highlights of my life. What a glorious day! We had gathered huge sprays of lilacs and white spirea to fill wicker baskets all over the gymnasium. (The baskets came from the funeral home, of course, and so did the paper fans and folding chairs.) It smelled absolutely heavenly in that gym, and the mixed chorus sounded divine.

Before the ceremony, we milled nervously about the home economics room, saying our good-byes to classmates, exchanging autographs or mementoes, wiping our eyes, and philosophizing briefly about the vast future ahead of us, how things would never be the same and how we would always miss and remember each other.

We were wrong on all counts. For the most part, the future never loomed vast. It unfolded one moment, one event at a time. Things went on about the same, except now we were making more of our own choices, so of course we made more mistakes. And although I loved them all dearly, I rarely thought again of Bertha Wininger, Toady Hurd, or Willard Branch. Nor they of me. We were soon busy enough with our own agendas.

During the ceremony, our parents shed a few tears. They were about to lose us, they thought, and things would never be the same. They were right that things would never be the same but wrong about losing us. You can't lose kids. Only the very spiritually mature can lose kids. For the rest of us, kids are like the other half of a Velcro unit. They glom on from time to time, and until we all outgrow our need for each other, the parents are glad to have them glom (but only for brief visits).

So that graduation was a joyous occasion and a very sad occasion. Later we forgot the sad part, the good-byes, when we discovered the joyous part of saying new hellos.

Every Body's Gotta Go

When seniors say they gotta go, they don't necessarily mean what they did in kindergarten when they said they hadda go. They might be telling you they're going and they're not coming back. More likely, they will slip out silently and without notice. But they will go. Every body's gotta go.

When the body goes is a closely guarded secret, rumored to be known to God alone, but I suspect God slips the information to at least a few souls who are very close to him. It could be whispered in the wind that blows over shady porches where the elderly rock, or shared in the night in a private conversation with a poor soul who lies in a coma because he is too petrified to let go.

In the case of my husband's grandmother, she knew. Grandma was ninety-seven, living in her own home in Wisconsin, when she called up all her children. "Come home," she said. "I'm going now."

Within hours, the remaining seven of her nine children were there with her, all of them in their seventies, along with other relatives. The only one who couldn't make it was her brother Ben from Oregon, who had fallen off the house that week while repairing the roof and had broken his knee. He was 102.

Grandma cooked a big meal and enjoyed having everyone there around her table once more. Then she lay down on the sofa for her afternoon nap, and of course she didn't wake up because she had told them, "I am going now," and she went.

My own grandmother wanted to go but couldn't find a way out. She entered a care center when she was ninety-three because she had fallen and broken her arm while cleaning her big, two-story house. She was in good health, however, and sharp of mind.

"Why would I want to stay on?" she asked as we sat together in the sunroom on one of my visits. There were few people in her new environment who could carry on a good conversation, and none of her friends were still alive to come by. Her husband was gone, her brothers and sisters were gone, as well as two of her three children. She could no longer see well enough to read or to sew, and frankly she was bored. But patiently she waited, spending her afternoons sitting on a sofa in that sunny common room, and it was here that she nodded off and left us at ninety-six when her name was called.

Her father had met his death in quite the opposite way. It came rushing toward him when he was in his early forties and caught up with him in the middle of town while he was driving his horse and buggy down the street. It struck him in the heart and ended his journey.

A few years ago, when my mother was ninety, she asked me to take her to a casino for the day. I expressed some concerns because she'd been having some heart problems, and I didn't want to take her too far from home or into an unhealthy environment or overstimulating activity. In my mind's eye, I pictured her sitting at a slot machine in a room full of ringing bells and smoke clouds, experiencing either complete exhaustion or the shock and commotion of a big win.

She looked at me for a long time, reading my thoughts, and then said, "Can you think of a better way to go?"

We went to the casino.

Darling, I Am Growing

We never say "I am old" or even "I am becoming old." We are always "growing old" because of our eternal optimism about the limitless future. But more than that, we think of ourselves as growing old because we are aware more than ever in our lives that we are, in fact, growing.

Not that we didn't learn our lessons as we went through life's experiences, but sometimes we were too busy to notice. Now we catch the missing links as we take time to regroup and as we watch the younger ones around us.

We are so proud when we see our children and grandchildren show courage and wisdom, when they are considerate and helpful to others, when they understand the values of hard work and self-reliance. "Well, they didn't learn it from the neighbors," someone will say, and that makes us feel we did a few things right. But of course the same is true if we see them make choices that bring hard consequences. We feel we must have put some bad information in their survival kit … and probably we did, if that's what we found in ours.

For me, the pain of growing is discovering that kind of chaff in the bottom of my own kit and seeing my mistakes become another's burden. At the same time, it reassures me that everyone is doing the best he can. If I had known better, I would have done it better. I would have passed on nothing but the best advice, the best tools, the best attitudes. Now I say, "If I had it do over again, I would do such and such." Hey, that is good. It's got to mean that I am learning and I am growing.

"So, what good is that going to do you?" asked my husband. "You've had your chance, and it's not coming around again."

"Oh, really?" I say, and smile as I go back to my counted cross-stitch and my counted blessings and my optimistic visions of a limitless future.

The Very Proper Pronoun

I'm sure you've never thought it odd
That Jesus Christ, the Son of God,
In gospel, prayer, in verse and hymn
Is always written He or Him,
While we and they are commonplace
And thee and thine are lowercase.

Then, have you ever wondered why
That me is me
But I am I?

From the Mountain

It has come to my attention
That you have spoken publicly
In words of praise,
Holding me up as one
Above all others,
One whose teachings
Are the only words of truth.

Now listen to the wind;
It is my patient sigh,
And know that even now
My eyes are rolling,
As the clouds.

Your opportunity
To learn and grow on earth
Is yours uniquely,
Never meant to be
Like every other.
The rules I sent to help you
Were just that … guidelines
To keep you safe from harm
Until you were mature enough
To set your own.

So get to work.
And do not worship
Those who gave you life
Or those who "saved" your life
But live the love and
Pass along the love
That is your life,
The love that was the message,
The love that is your hope.

Promise Lands

It's not that I don't believe
There is order in the universe
And a greater intelligence
That set the plan in motion and
Oversees its course,
Not that I don't believe
A special being with a lifeline
To the creator came, not once
But many times, to many people
With a simple message: love.

It's more that I don't believe
In the entities formed to organize
My belief, to reinforce it with
A weekly retelling of the story,
(Along with a few poems and
Clever asides, with references to
Scribes and scholars who quoted those
Who quoted those before them,
Followed by another song,
A blessing, and coffee
In the vestibule).

It's not that I don't believe
These things are good for those
Who need reminding, need the
Comfort, the support, and fellowship.

It's more that I don't think
They get it, or they would have
Graduated, gone into the world
To pass it on and leave the seats
To fill with unbelievers who
Have yet to hear the word.

It's not that I don't accept
The many systems that exist,
Like ours, to carry on the message
Of their messenger, to build a culture
Based on faith and
Hope for better things.

It's more, I'm thinking now, that
They, like we, while answering
The worship call so faithfully
And following the rules
To qualify and lock in all
Rewards and benefits of paradise
May wonder now just when
And just exactly how
We lived in opportunity
And lost the peace on earth.

Looking Back ... Looking Forward

When I was a child, I believed in angels, and I believed in fairies, not because they left money under my pillow in exchange for a baby tooth but because "something" was there with me whenever I walked through my mother's flower garden or climbed into the mulberry tree to eat the ripe fruit and listen to the birdsongs. "Something" spoke to me of everything around me, drawing my attention to the tiniest details ... the dew on the petal of a rose, the ants in their comings and goings, the sounds of newborn calves, the feel of the winter snowstorm. Life was all around me, I was part of it all, and I was never alone.

Looking back, I realize that if I lost this sense of connection at times through the years, so steeped with the business of living and surviving, it was there nevertheless, and no doubt I had the backing of my angels in every direction I turned, every good decision I made. Now, approaching my leisure years, I again feel their touch and share with them the precious moments of living.

Now I know that my helpers had not left and returned, rather that I had left and returned. And I'm fairly certain that I did receive their help and support through all the years in good ideas that "just came to me," in the certainty of my decisions, in chance meetings with opportunity, and in occasions of surprising serendipity.

My Prayer

My own true inner self, light of my life and source of my being, that part of me that is whole and complete and yet so veiled and dimly understood I don't know what to call you,

Shine upon my life and open up a new world for me; send your infinite wisdom into the darkest corners of my universe to light the way and rule with understanding love,

So that everything I say and do and every condition that manifests about me may be a reflection of the highest spiritual life within.

May I seek daily through meditation and living experience those personal insights that are food for my spiritual growth, remembering always my forgiveness lies within. I do not judge but accept myself just as I am, knowing I must learn from day to day and release the past that brought the learning.

Nor do I judge my fellow man but accept him as he is and free him to his own path, his own learning.

May I never exist in the ego alone but realize with all souls and all things a oneness in spirit from which I can never be separated.

For the plan of my life is known to you alone, with all potential for good, larger than I can see at any one moment, in my eternal now.

So be it.

Thank you for allowing me to share with you. If you enjoyed this book and would like to order more for gifts, you can do so through bookstore. iuniverse.com or amazon.com. While there, I'd appreciate a positive book review if you did, in fact, enjoy the read. You may also find this book in Barnes and Noble and other bookstores.

If you have comments or want to share an insight with me, please e-mail me at this address: sharinglife89@gmail.com. I would love to hear from you.

My blog, which I prefer to call My Notebook, is at http://mymarkland.wordpress.com.